AMAZING
EYE TRICKS

A M A Z I N G
EYE TRICKS
-YOU WON'T BELIEVE YOUR EYES-

Gary W. Priester and Gene Levine

Published and distributed by
TOBAR LIMITED
The Old Aerodrome, Worlingham, Beccles, Suffolk,
NR34 7SP, UK
www.tobar.co.uk

This edition printed 2010

© 2006 Arcturus Publishing Limited

Printed in China

ISBN: 978-1-903230-28-2
AD000044EN

Contents

How to view stereograms

This is intended as a guide for viewers who have never seen stereogram 3D effects, and for those viewers who are a bit rusty. Please don't be discouraged if you can't visualize the effects right away. After all, what you are doing is overcoming a lifetime habit of viewing everything with 'normal' stereovision: that which gives us a sense of depth in our everyday viewing of the world.

First, let's try using a physical aid. After that are some practices for viewing autostereograms (stereograms that work without physical aids).

To view hidden-image and stereo-field stereograms, you cannot use normal, or cross-eyed vision (see fig. 1). Instead, you have to use parallel vision, which is what you will do automatically if you place a piece of card between your eyes when viewing the images (see fig. 2).

Unlike cross-eyed vision, there is no strain or discomfort with parallel vision. The essential key, in fact, is to relax your eyes into viewing this way.

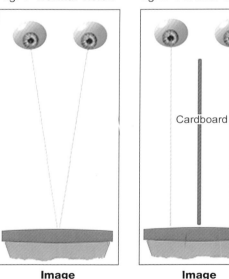

fig. 1 **Normal vision**   fig. 2 **Parallel vision**

Cardboard

Image   Image

Top view

Below is a stereo-pair image. Place the card directly in the middle of the pair, as illustrated in fig. 2. Now move your head to position the other end of the card between your eyes. Disregard focusing for now.

A stereo-pair

If the alignment is good, you should see only one image. Now relax your eyes, and slowly bring things into focus, pulling your head back. Remember, you should not think you see a 3D effect; you should know for sure. When you are sure, hold that focus and remove the card. You should now see three images: the one in the middle containing the 3D effects.

Congratulations, you are now viewing a stereogram as it should be seen!

Continue with the practices without aids, opposite. The only thing you'll need here is two eyes. Let go of the normal way you focus on something on a page. Let your eyes relax.

Viewing practice for autostereograms

Practice 1

The objective here is to let your mind process these two objects until they appear as three. Let your eyes relax, and move your head forward or away until three zeros appear clearly.

Your primary inclination is to focus on the above two objects in the normal way. But now, look behind them; look behind the page and forget about focusing. Try this for a while until you gradually see the three zeros.

When you see a non-existent object appear between the two existing ones, you have mastered the basis of the stereo-pair. It is in the centre object where the 3D effect takes place. This is the crux of autostereograms.

So where does the centre image come from?

It is helpful to remember that visual perception happens in the brain, not the eyes. What we're doing here is fooling the brain. The eyes are feeding it visual information, but not in the usual manner, and so the mind gives us a middle object. And if you introduce some subtle offsets and distortions into two otherwise similar images, the mind will perceive depth even though it is not truly there.

If you view three objects as an autostereogram, you should perceive four objects. Four objects will look as if they are five, and so on.

Practice 2

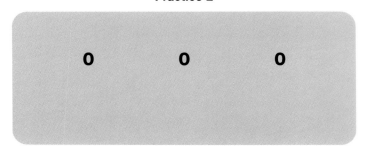

And now for some 3D:

Between these two objects, another object should appear with the smaller square floating over the larger.

Practice 3

Still can't see it?

Pull back, and focus normally on the centre object of the three below. Now lean slowly forward into the page, holding that focus until it is broken or you see four objects, clearly.

Master these practices, and you should have no problem moving on to fully-fledged autostereograms.

Practice 4

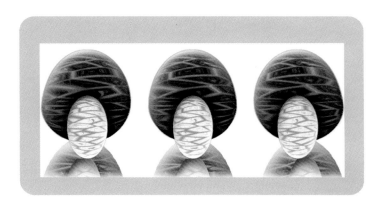

© 2003 GENE LEVINE

© 2003 GENE LEVINE

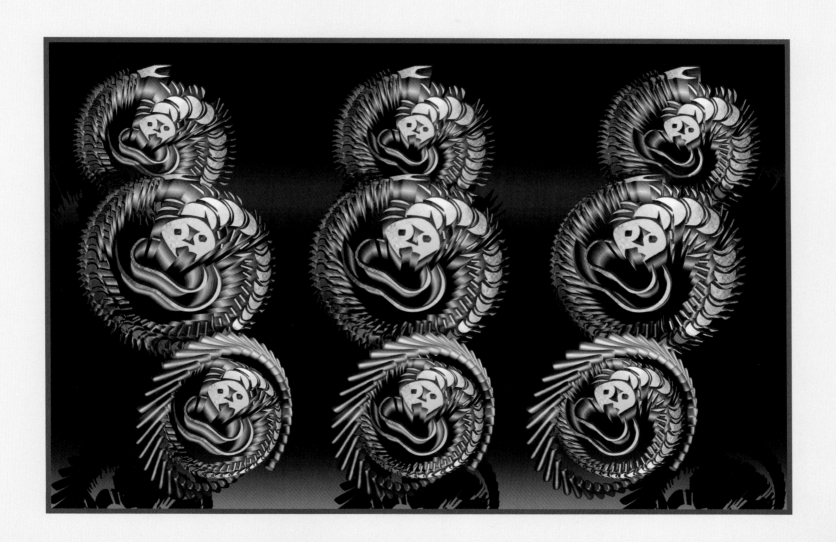

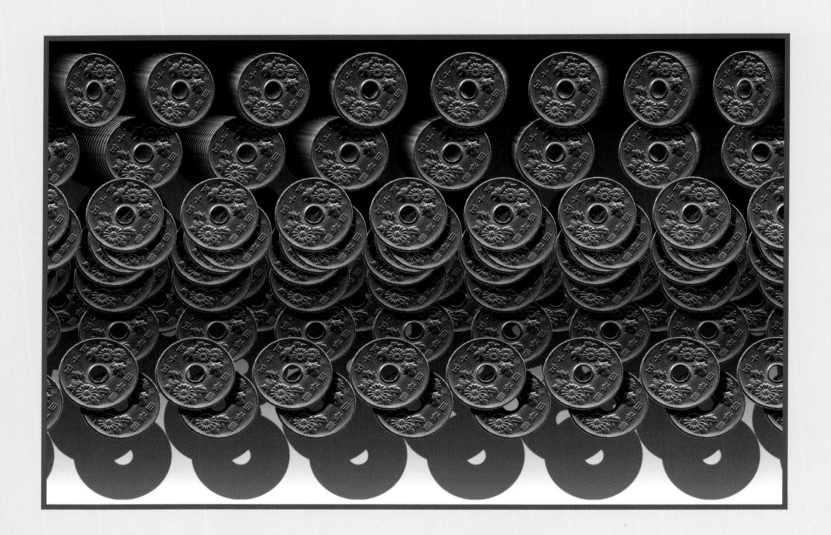

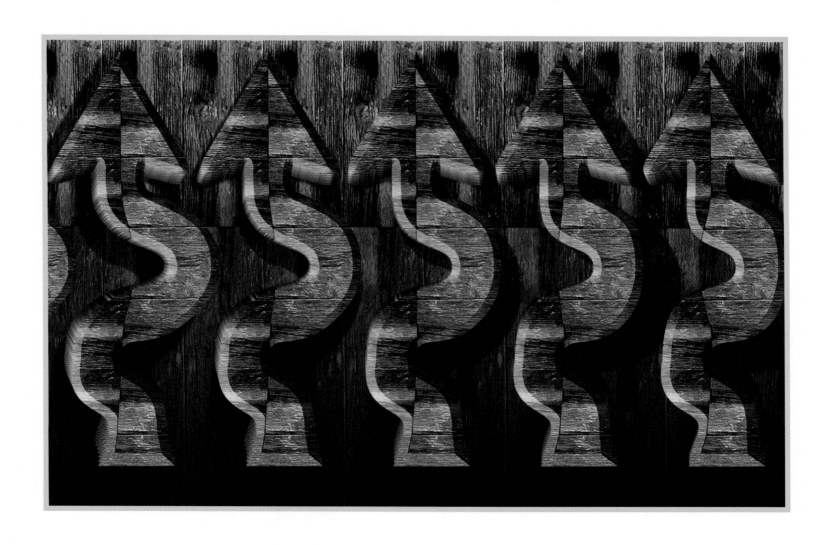

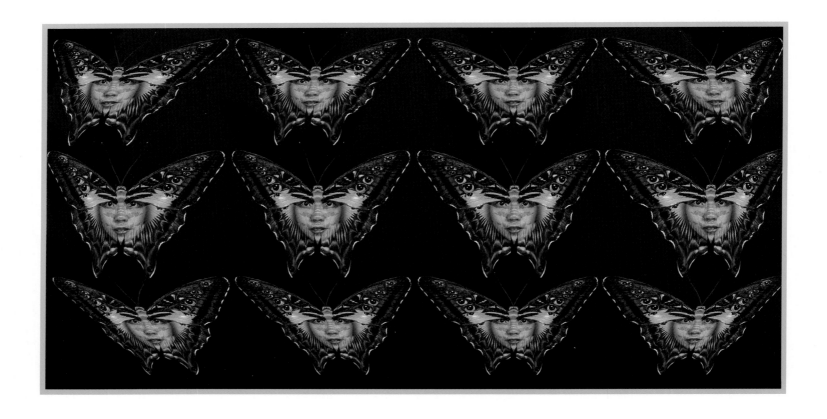

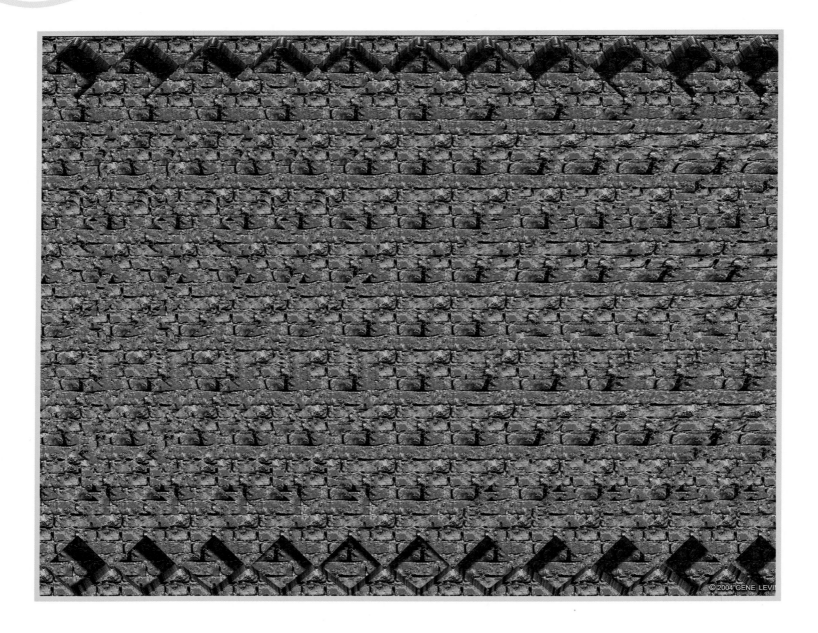

© 2004 GENE LEVI

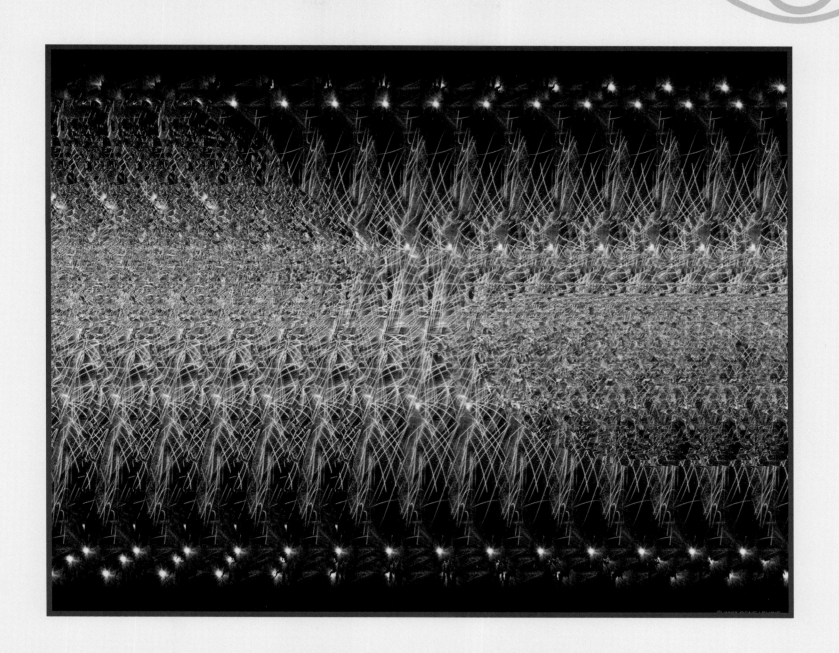

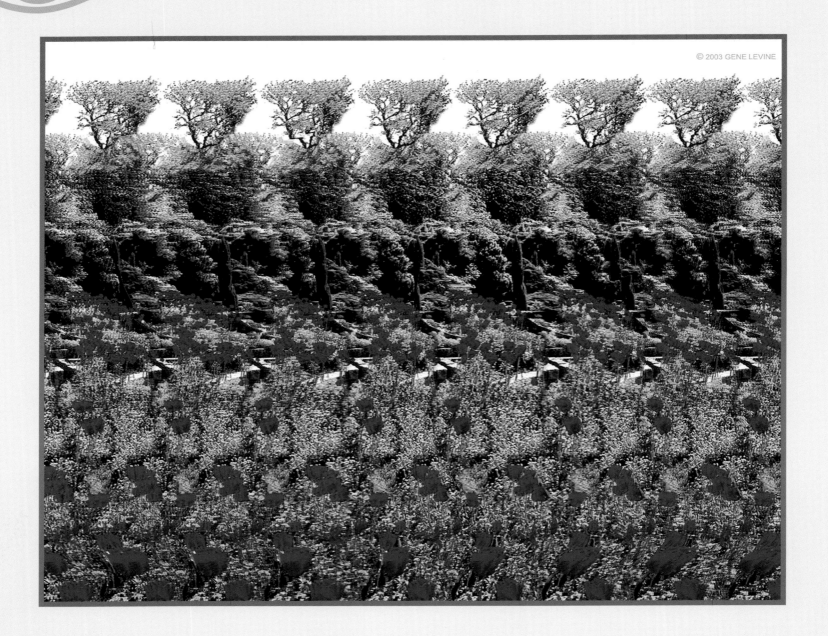

© 2003 GENE LEVINE

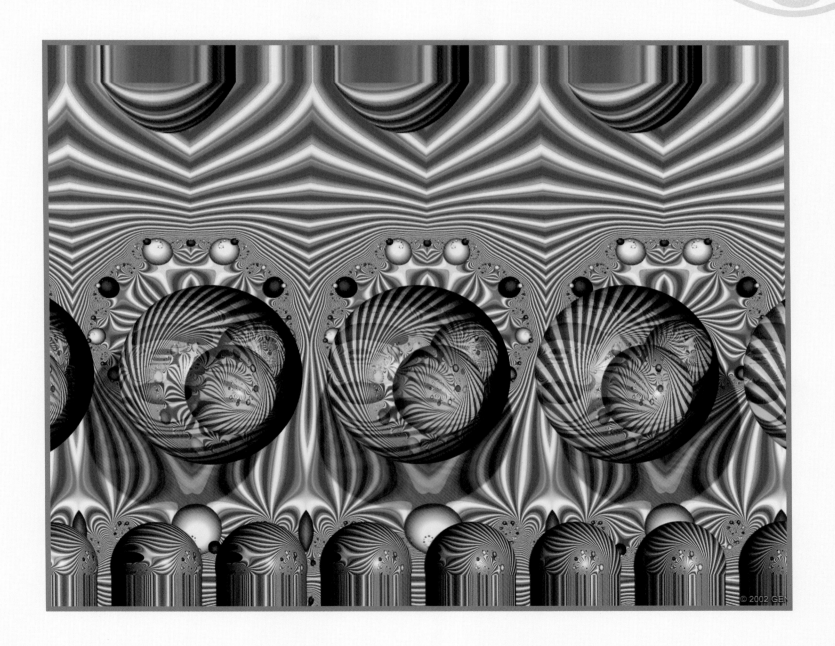

© 2002 GEN

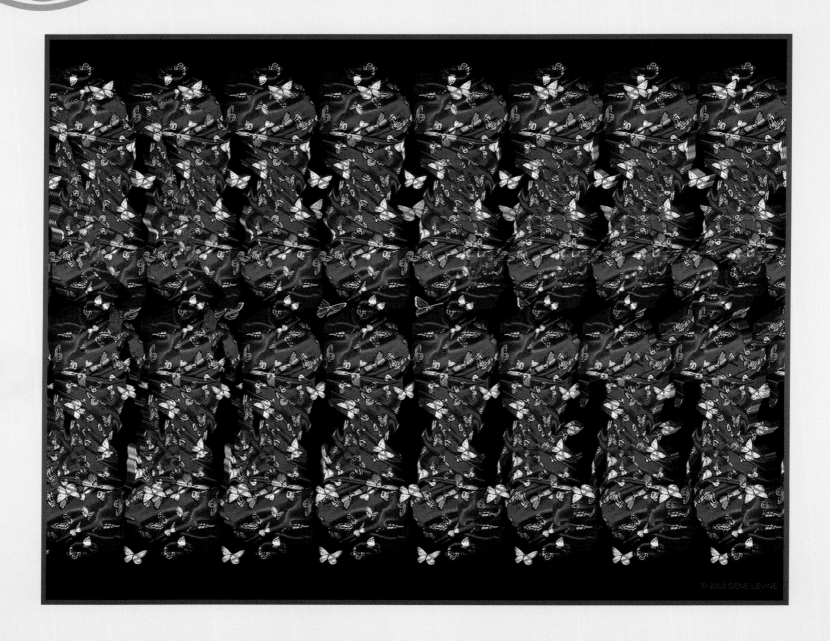

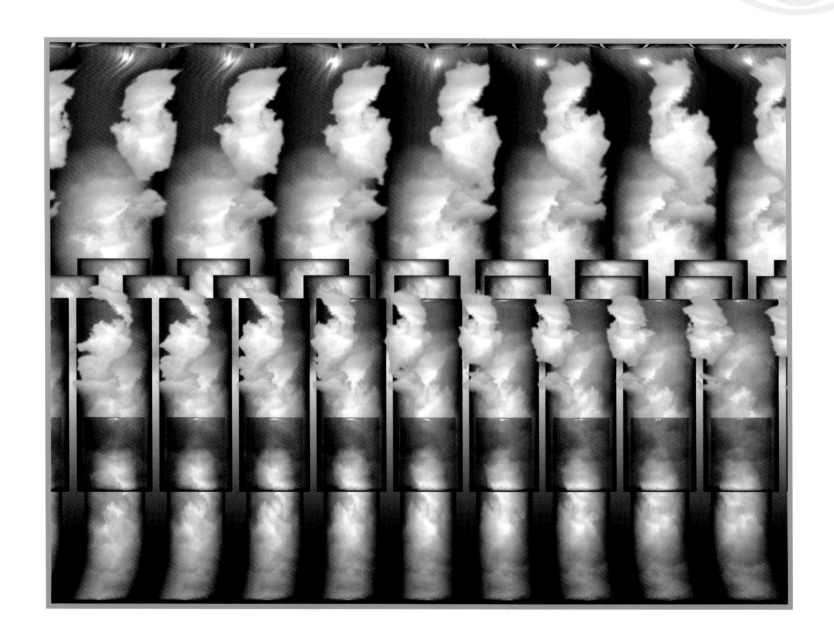

Colour Sieve

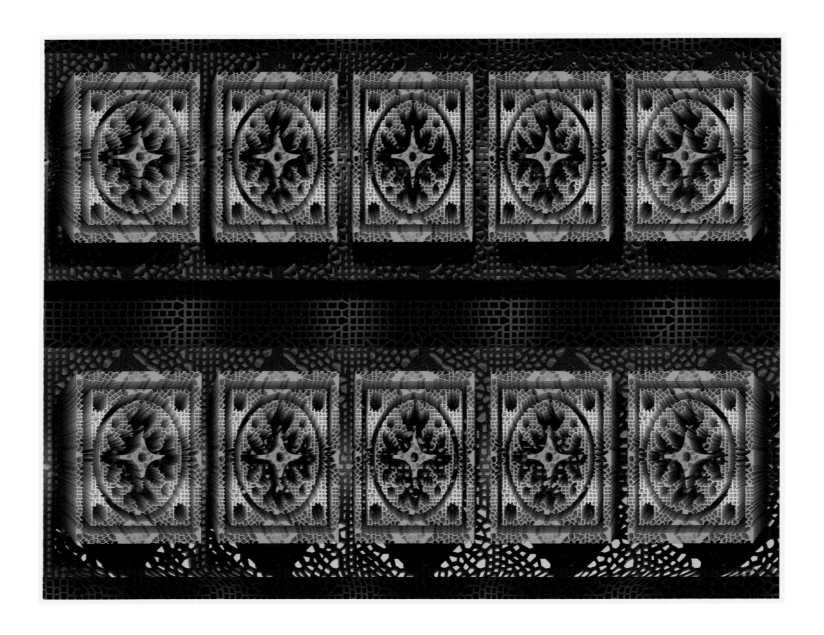

© 2003 GENE LEVINE

© 2003 GENE LEVINE

Mixed Vegetables

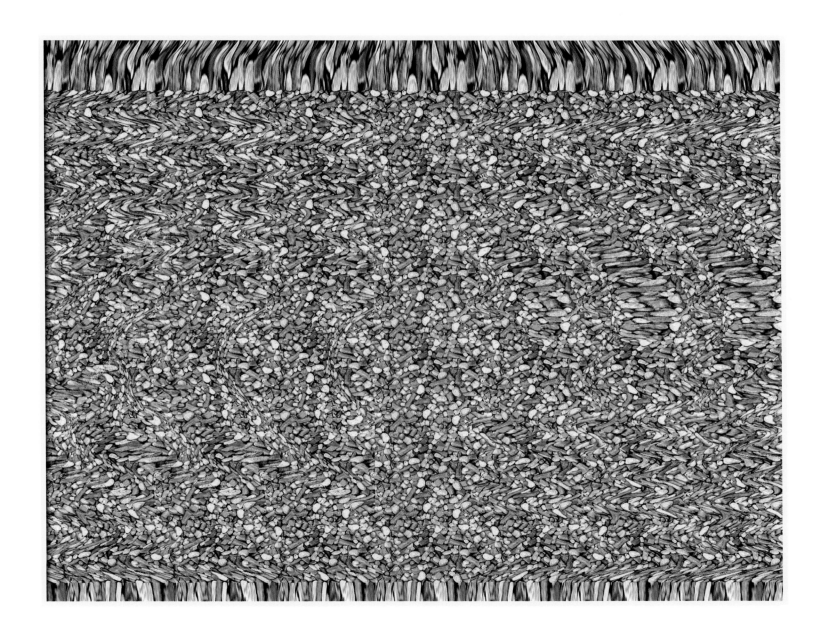

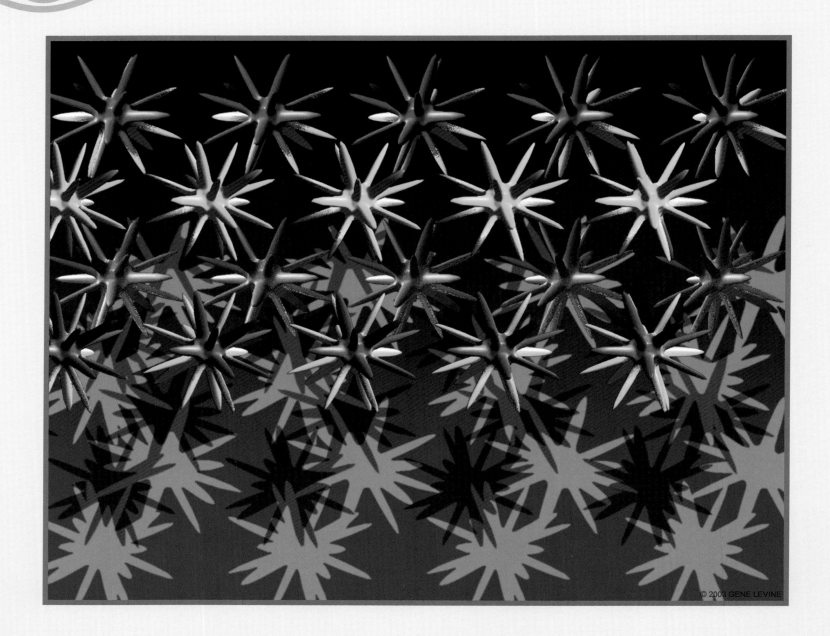

© 2003 GENE LEVINE

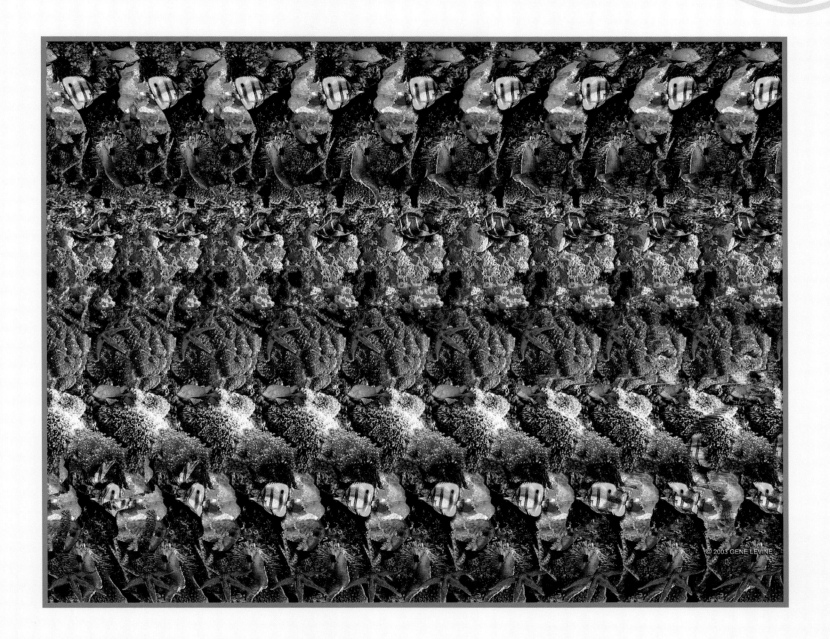

© 2003 GENE LEVINE

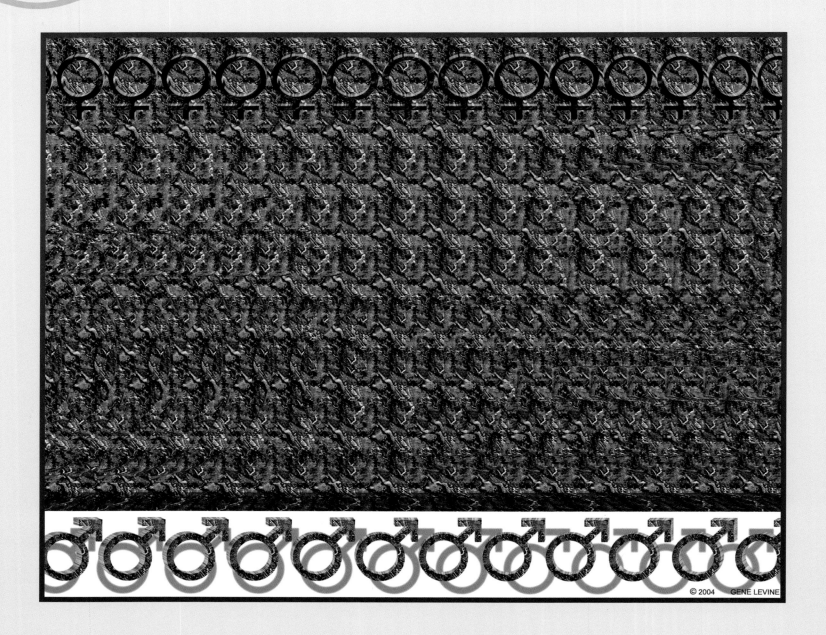

© 2004   GENE LEVINE

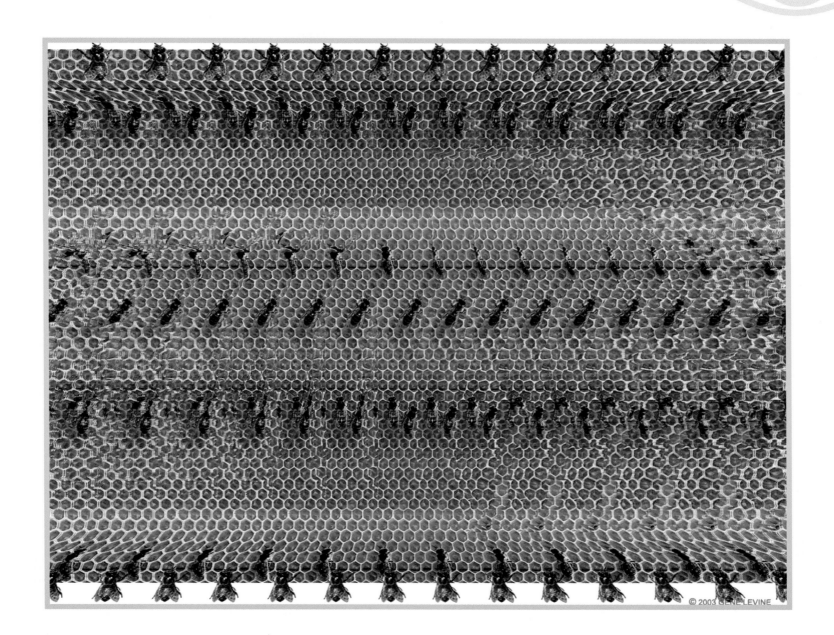

© 2003 GENE LEVINE

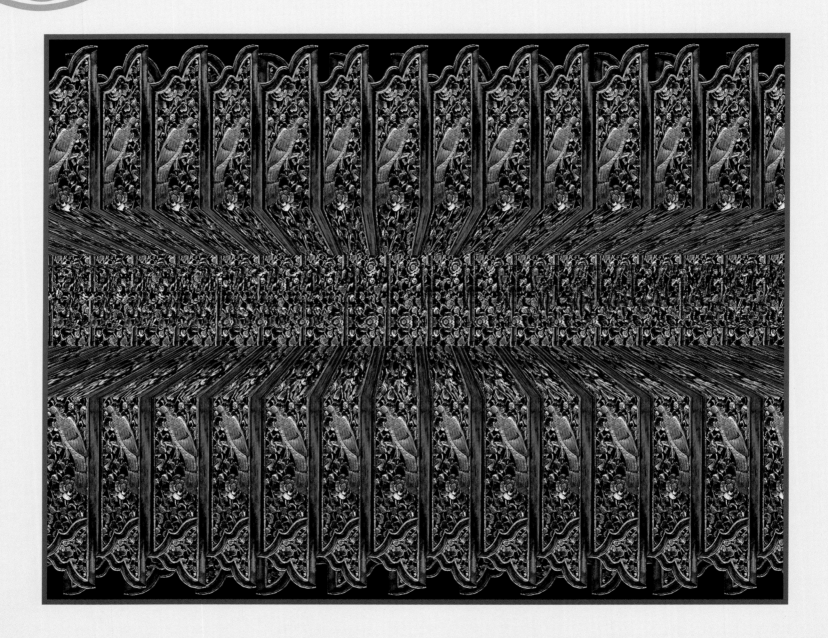

©2003 GENE LEVINE

Fireworks

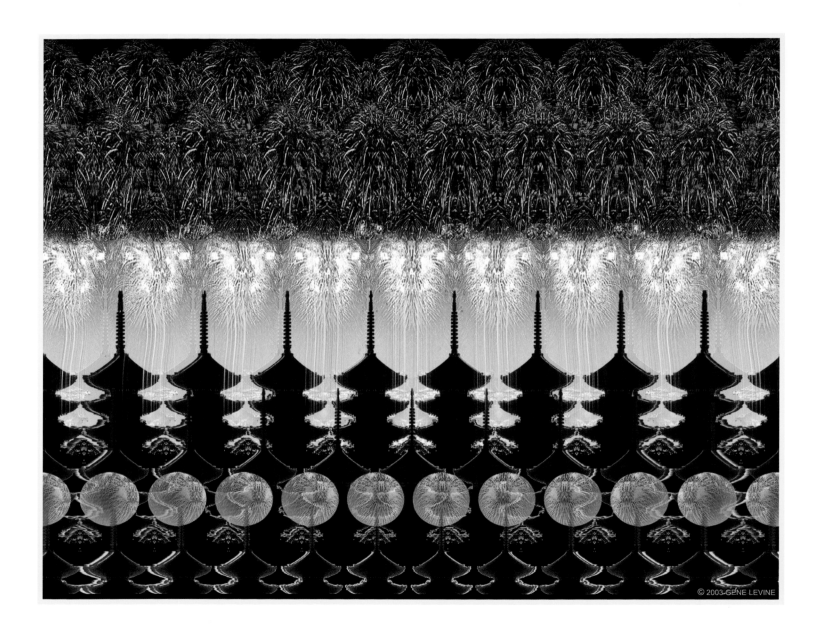

© 2003 GENE LEVINE

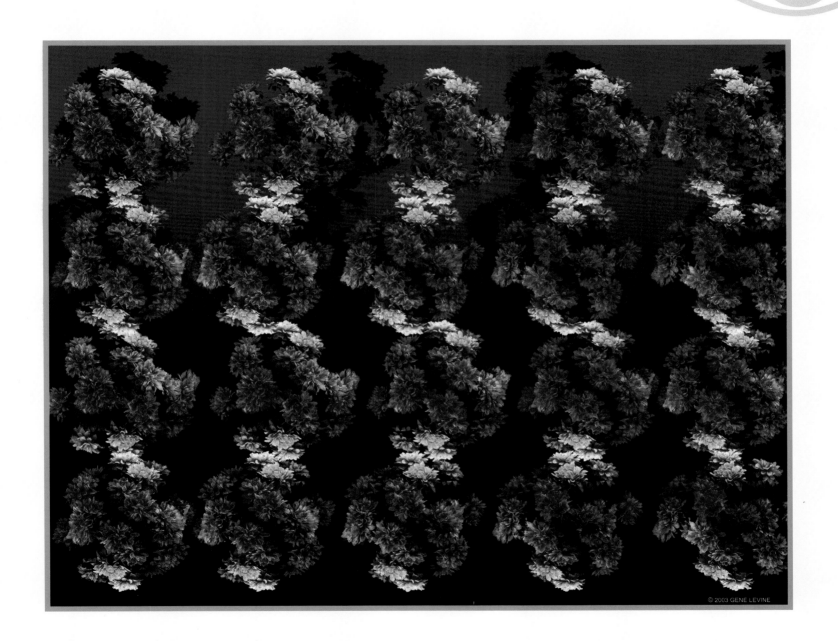

© 2003 GENE LEVINE

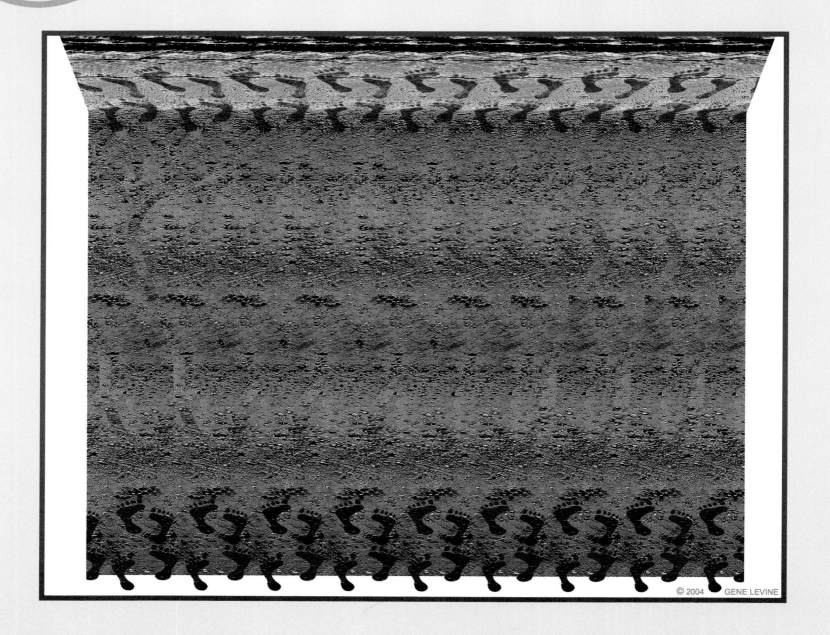

© 2004 GENE LEVINE

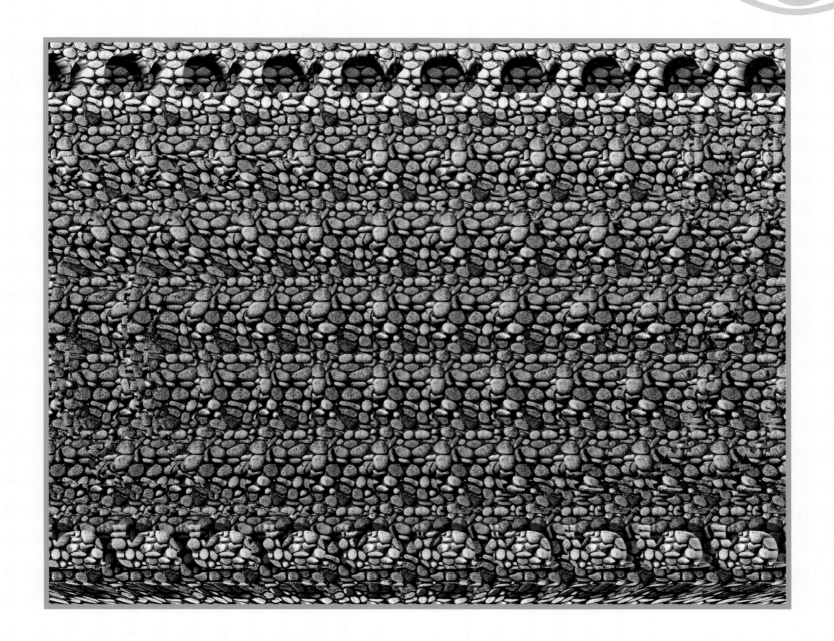

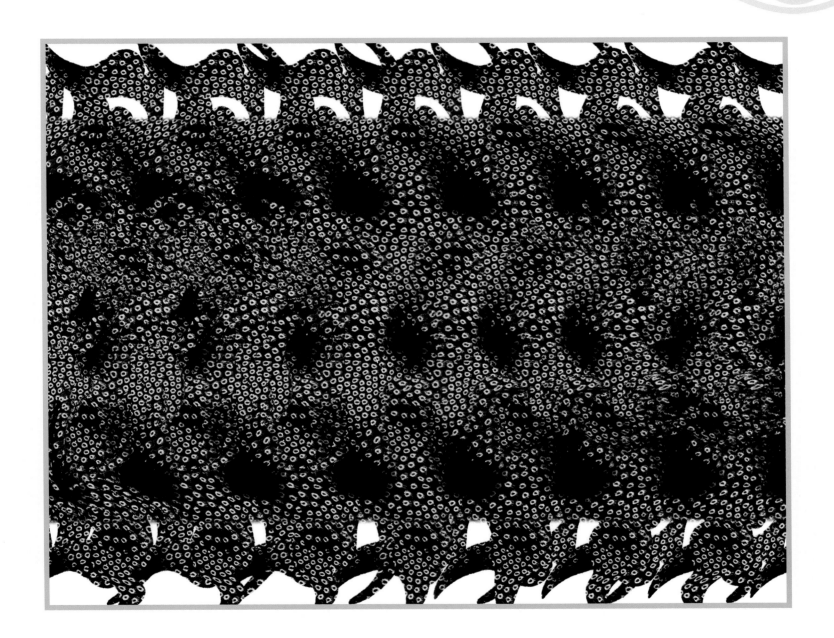

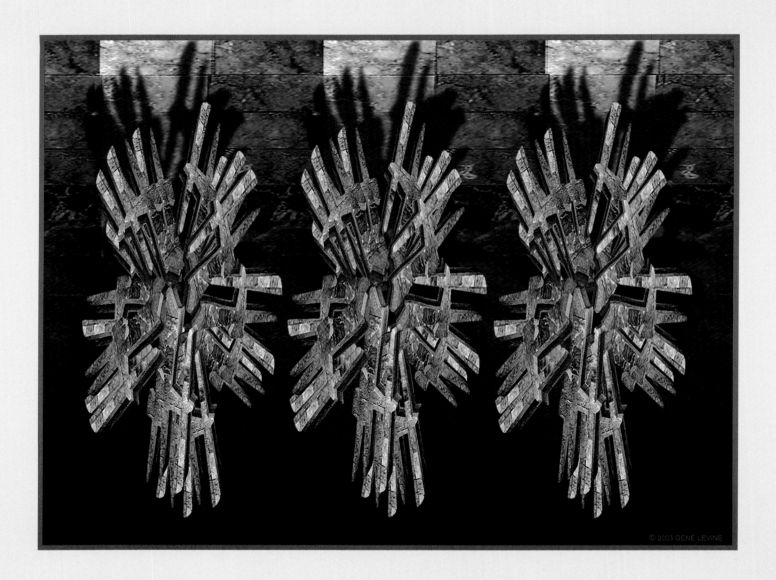

© 2003 GENE LEVINE

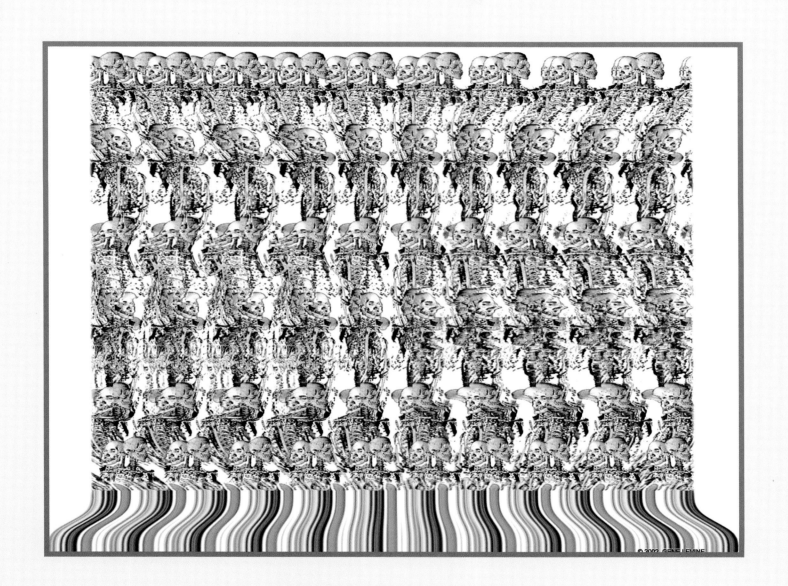

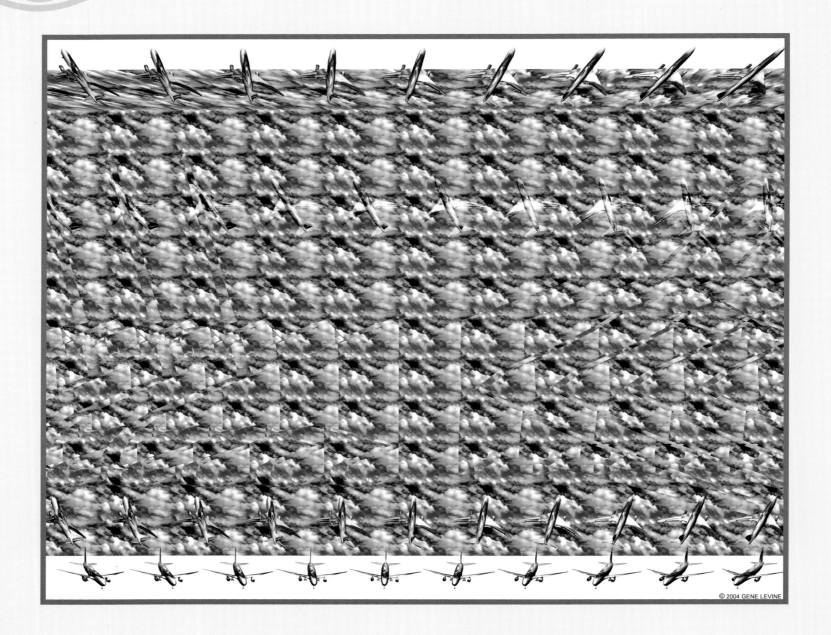

© 2004 GENE LEVINE

© 2001 GENE LEVINE

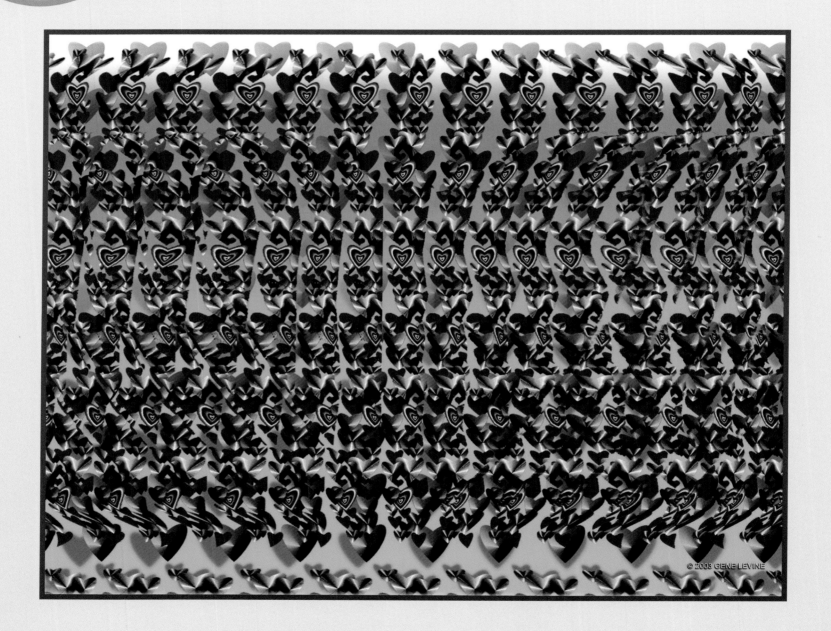

© 2003 GENE LEVINE

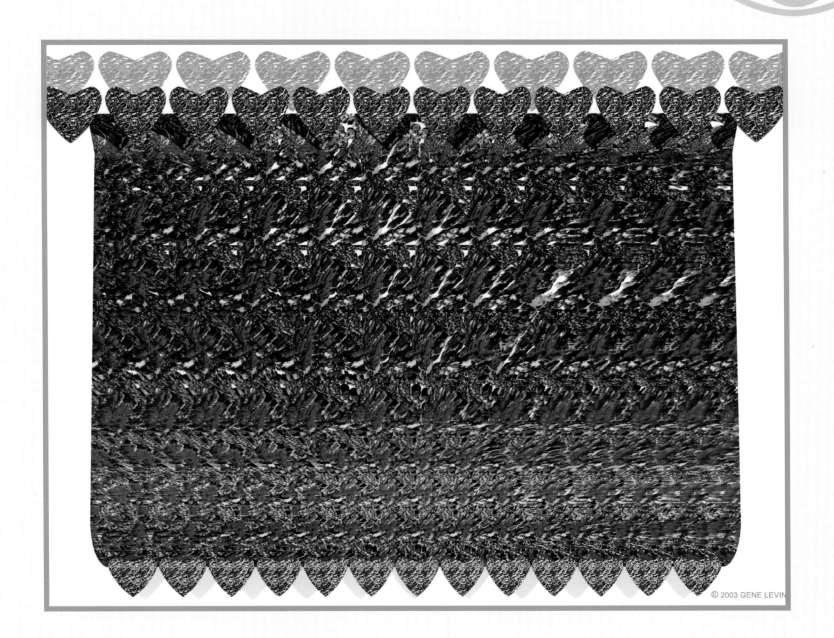

© 2004 GENE LEV

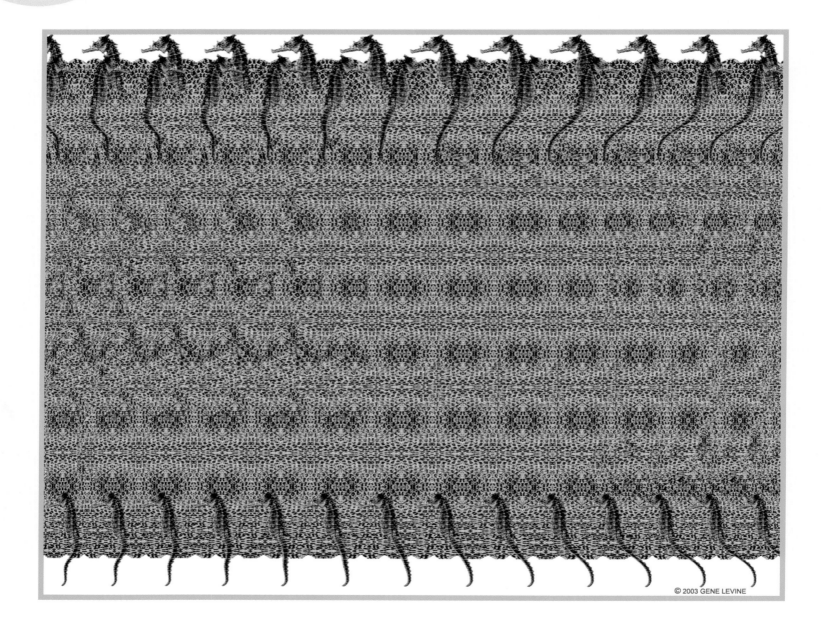

© 2003 GENE LEVINE

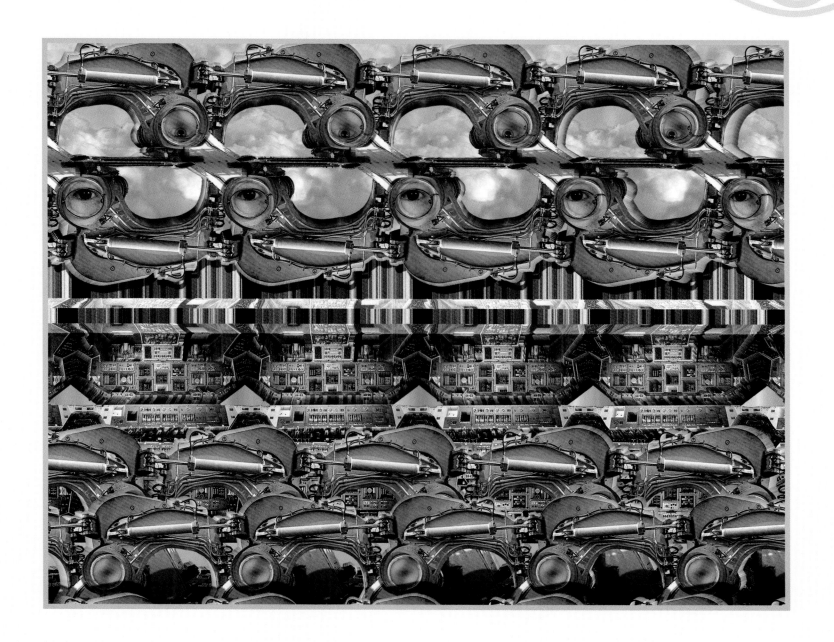

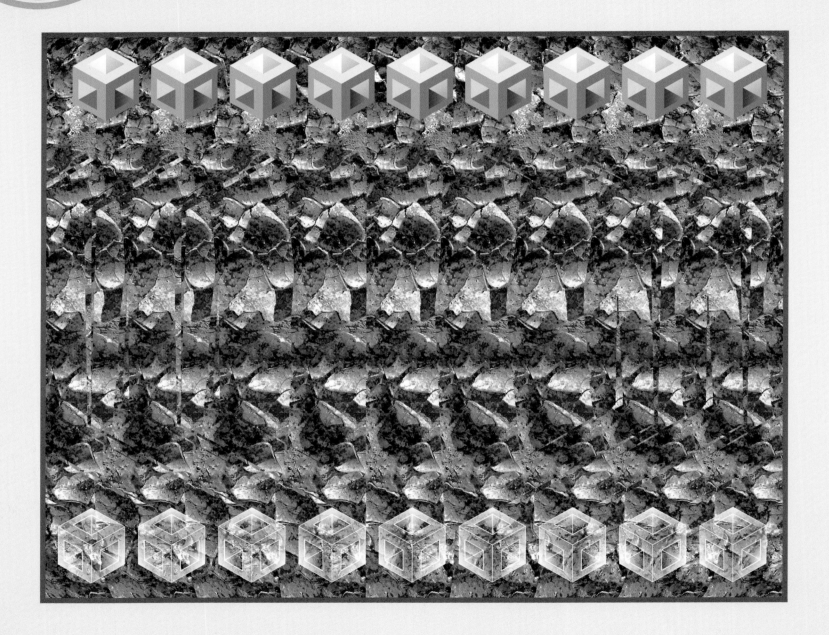

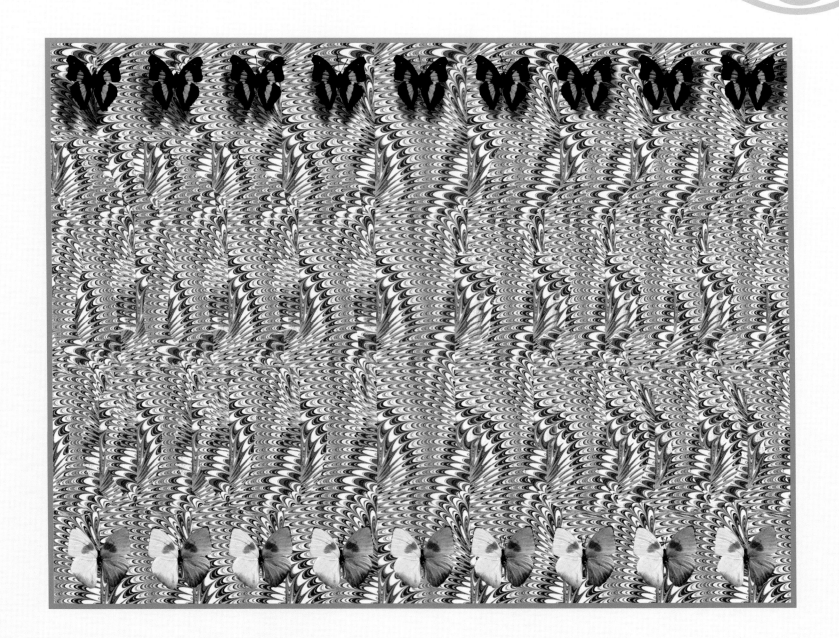

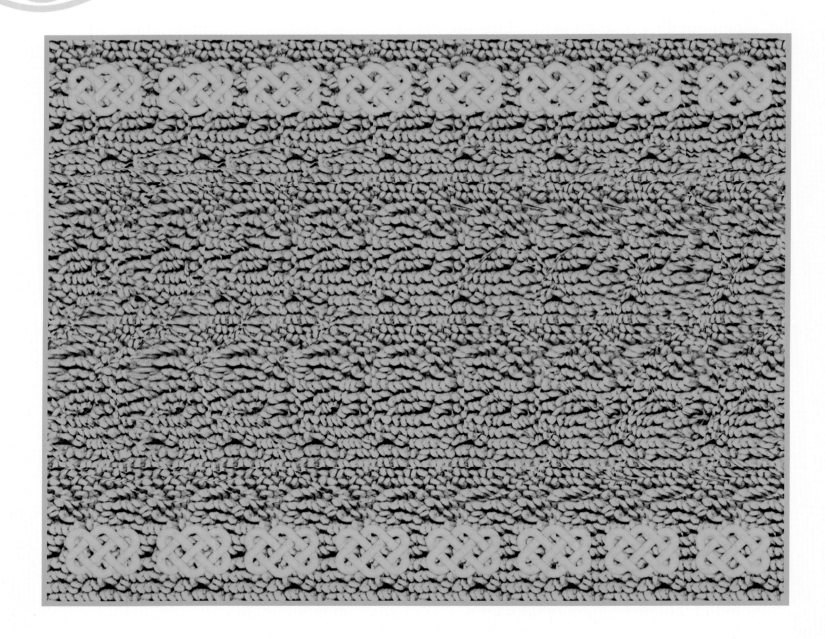

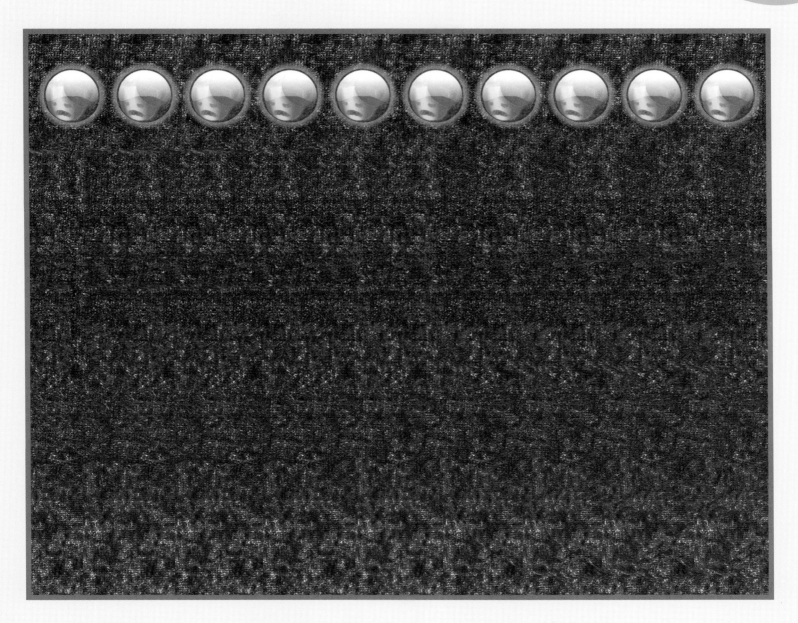

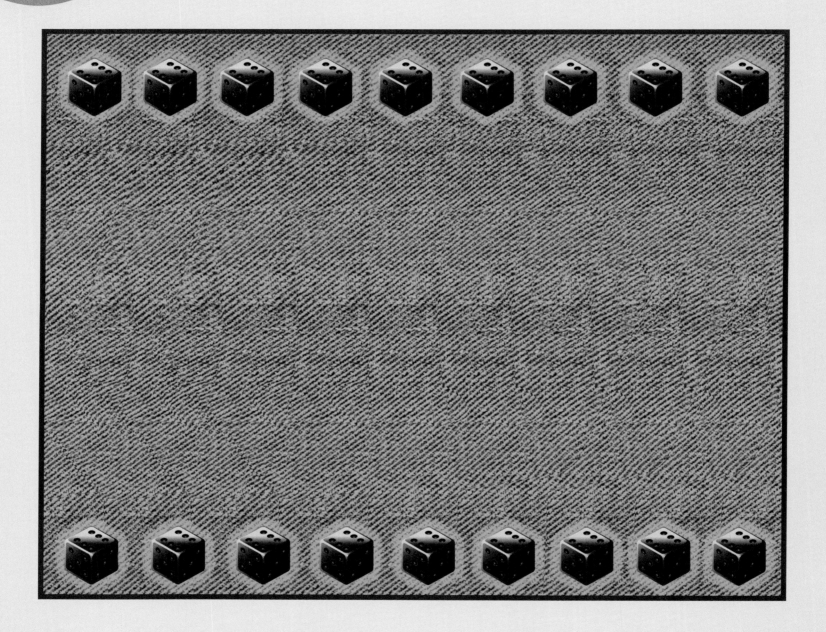

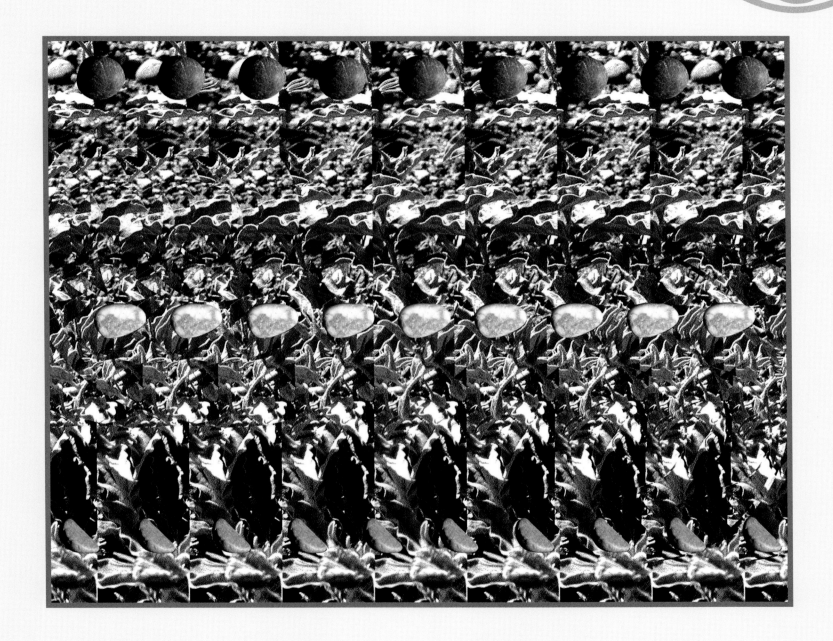

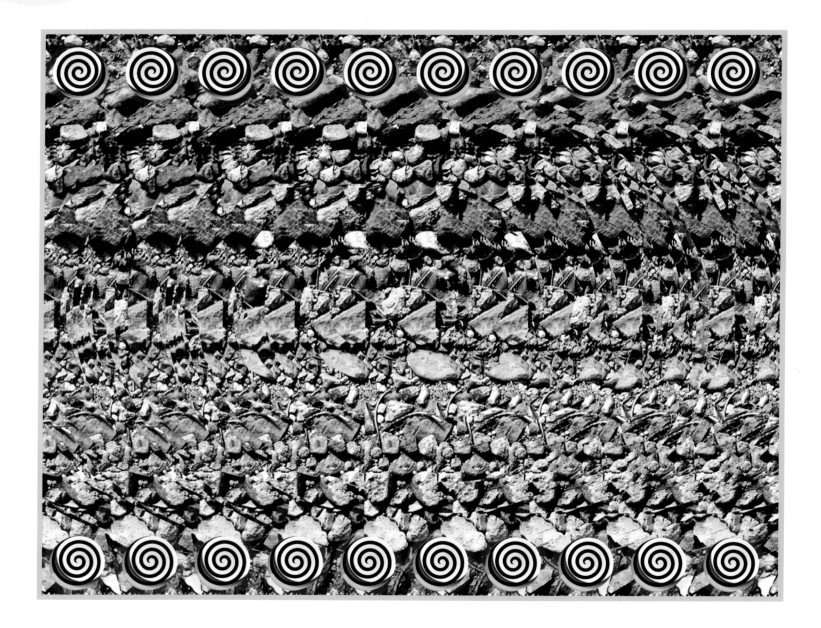

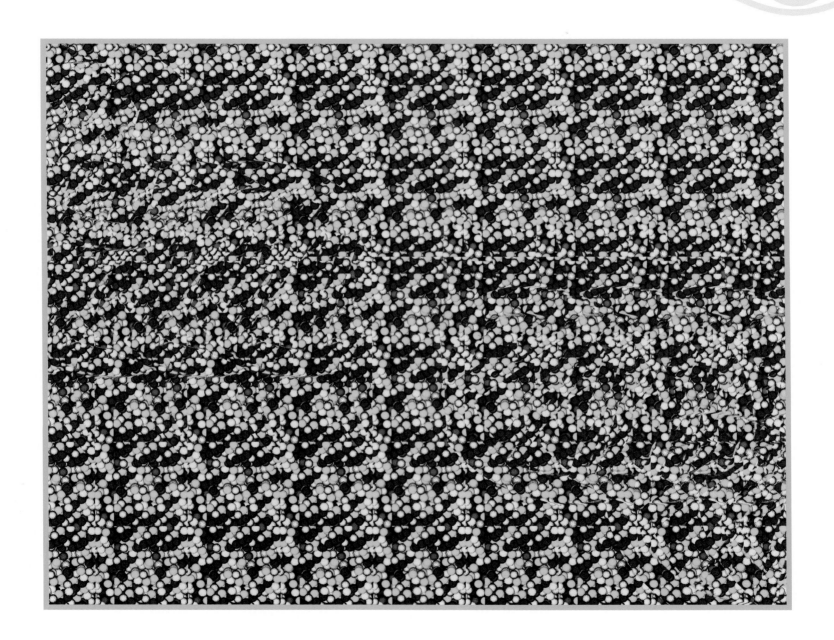

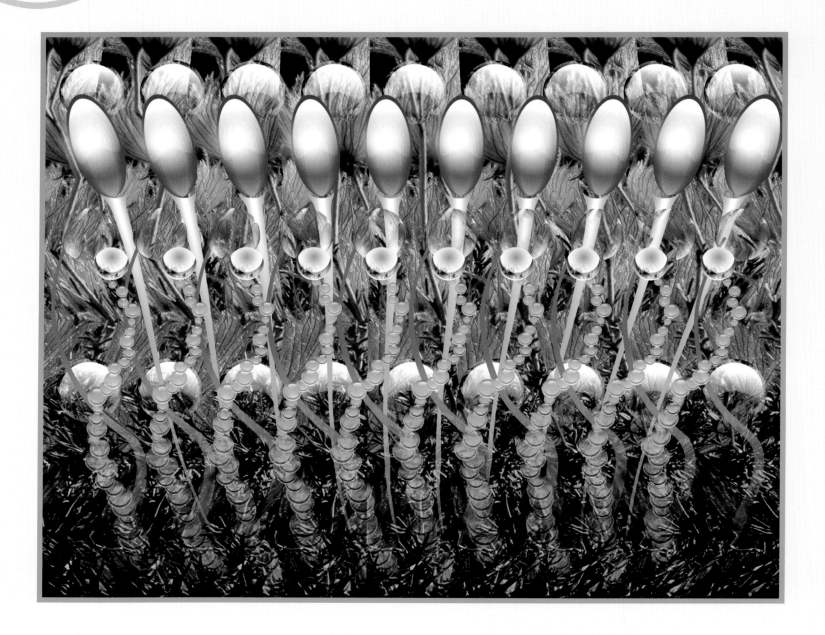

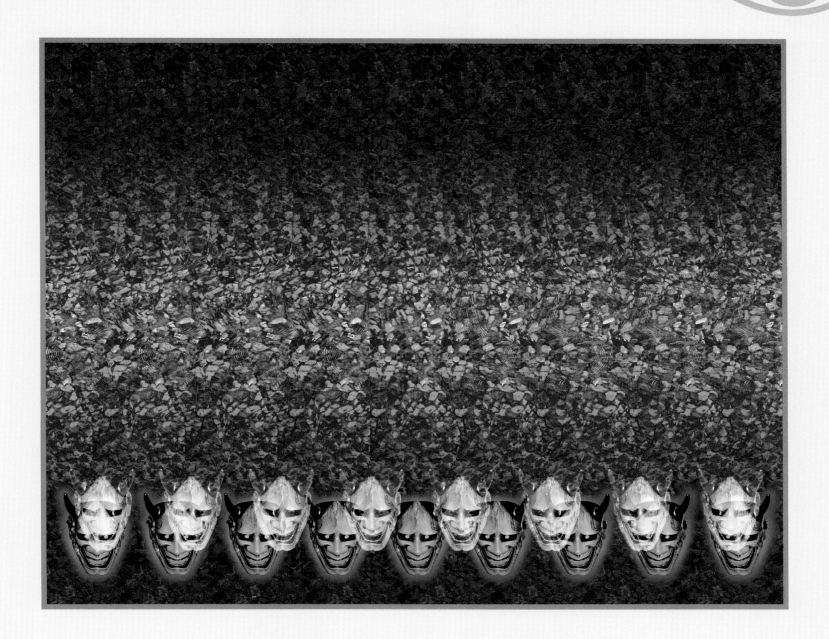

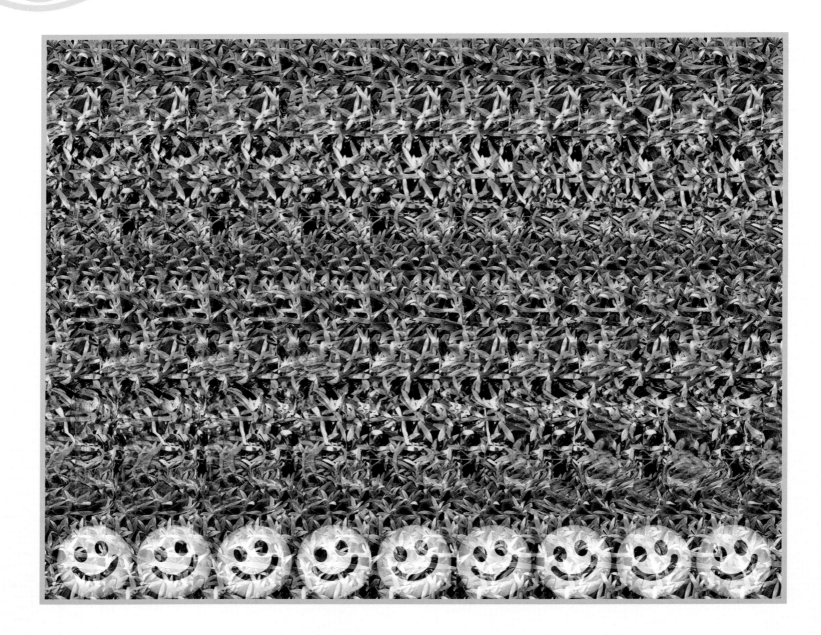

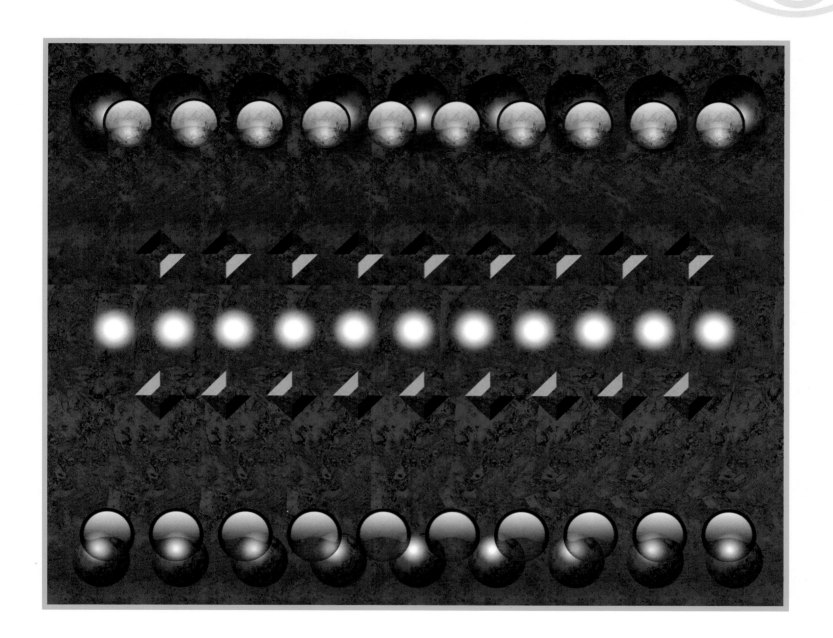

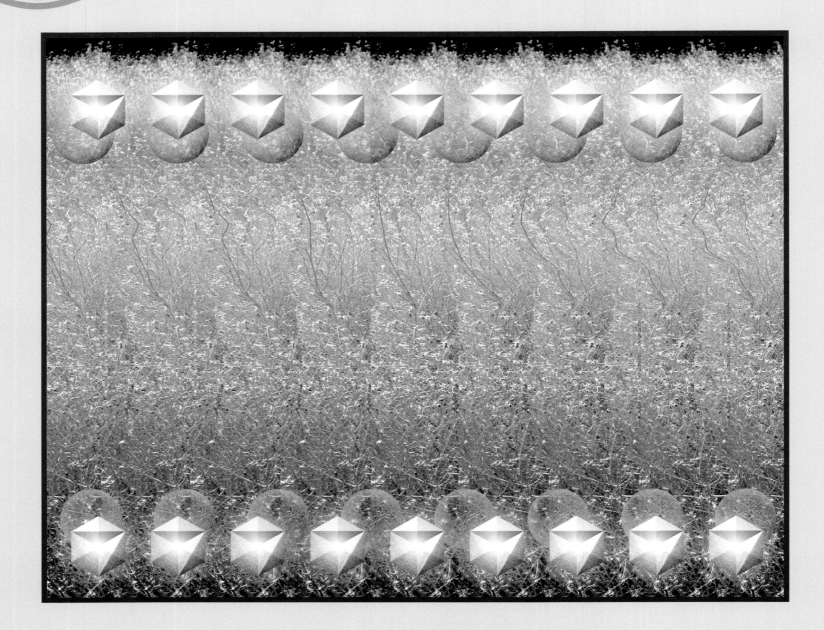

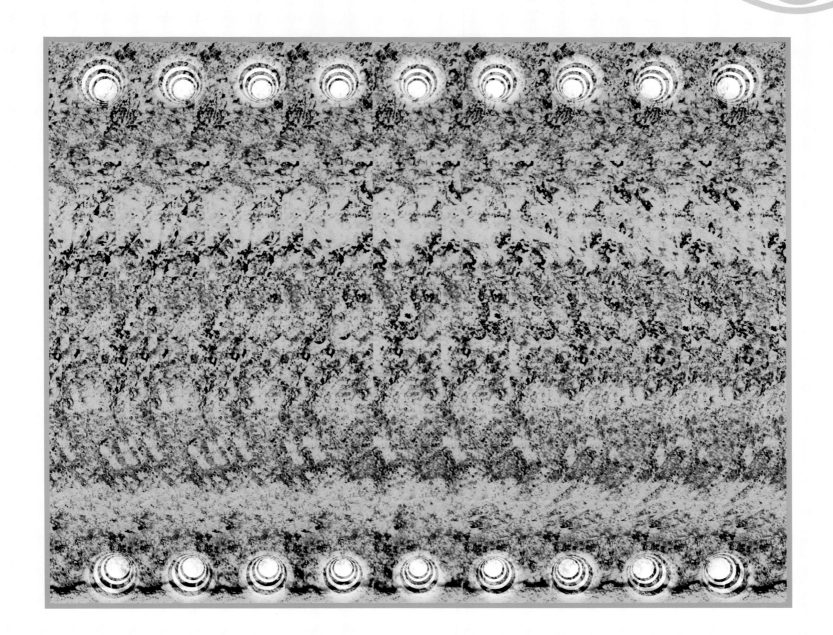

Lock & Key

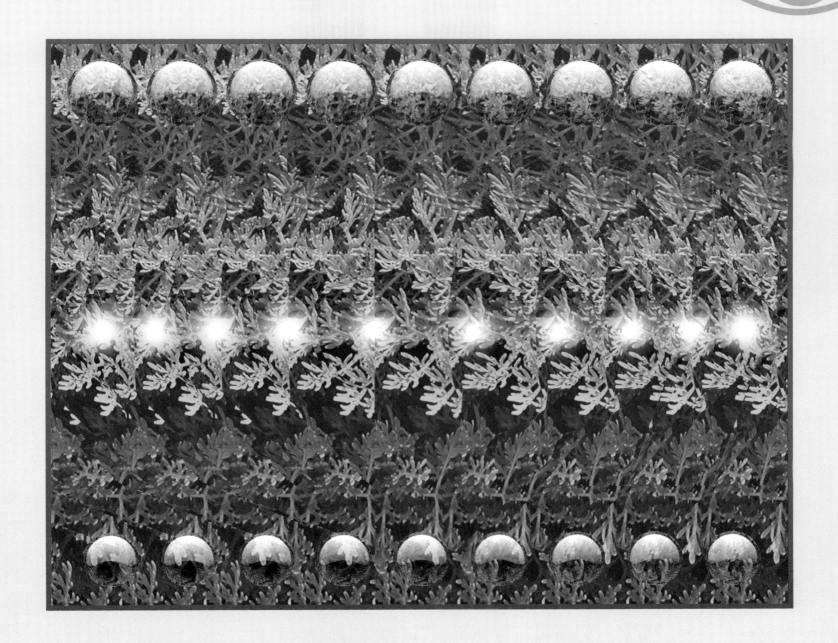

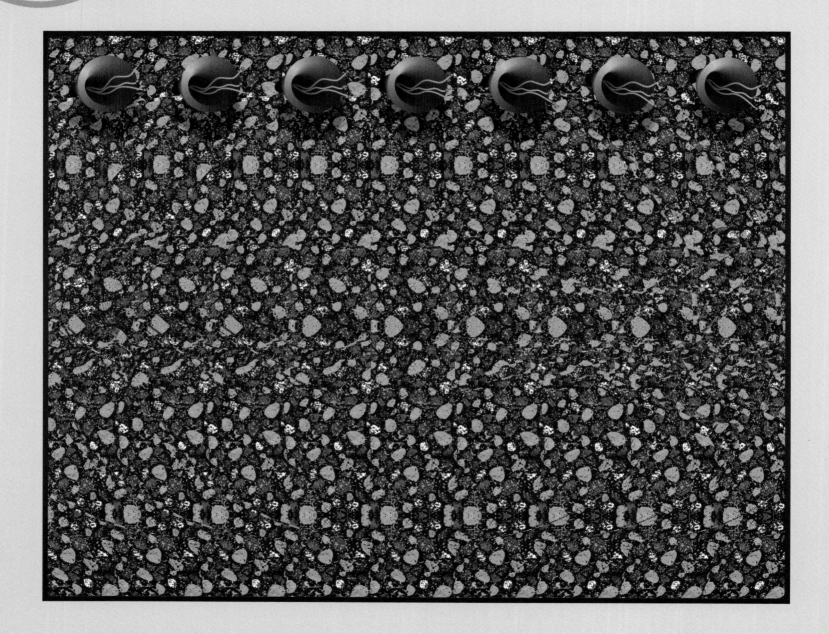

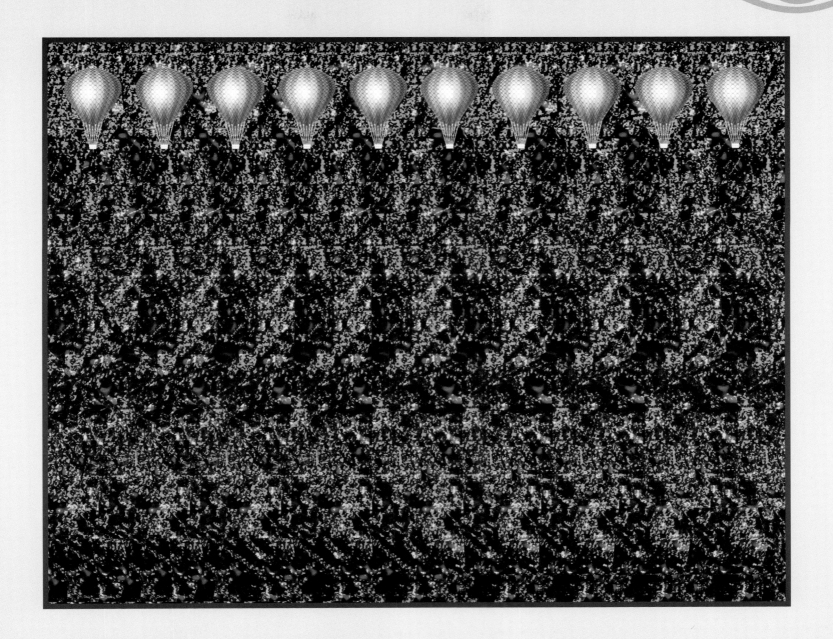

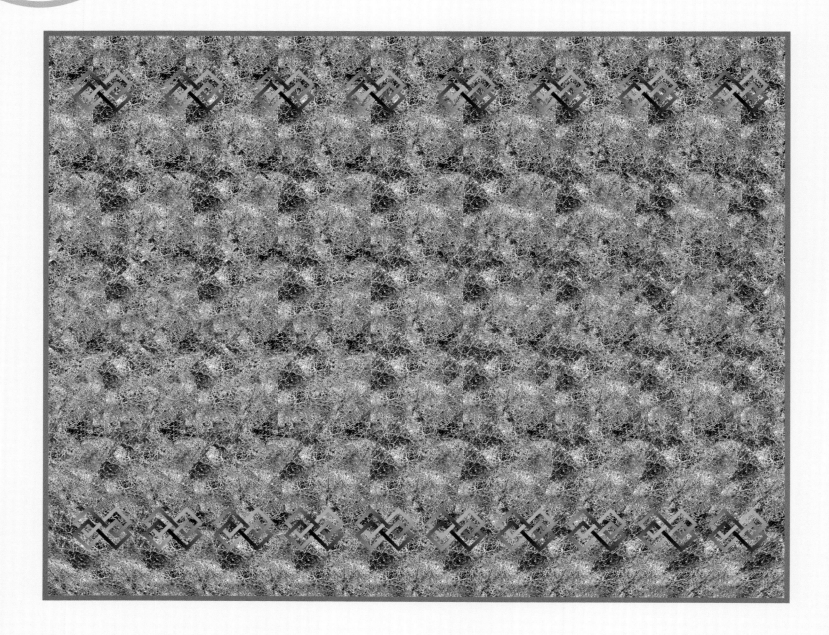

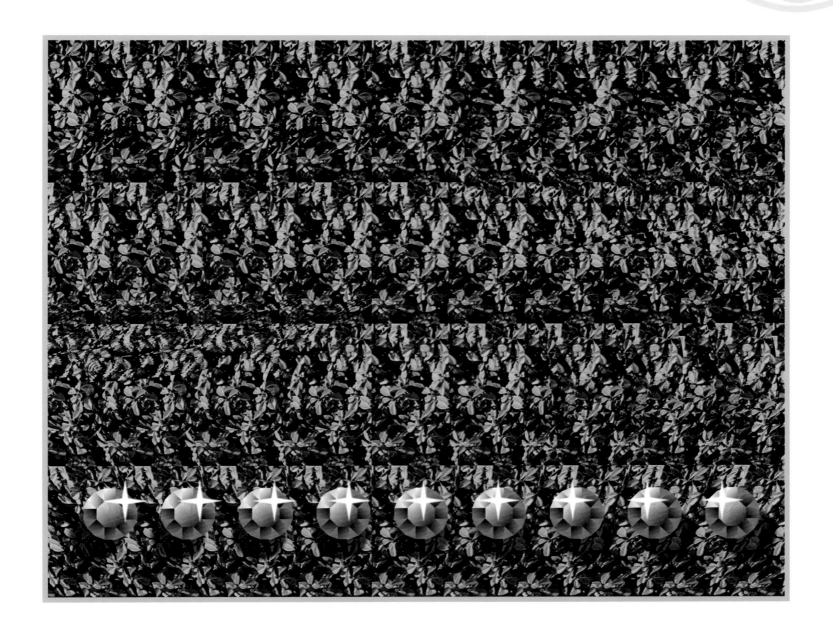

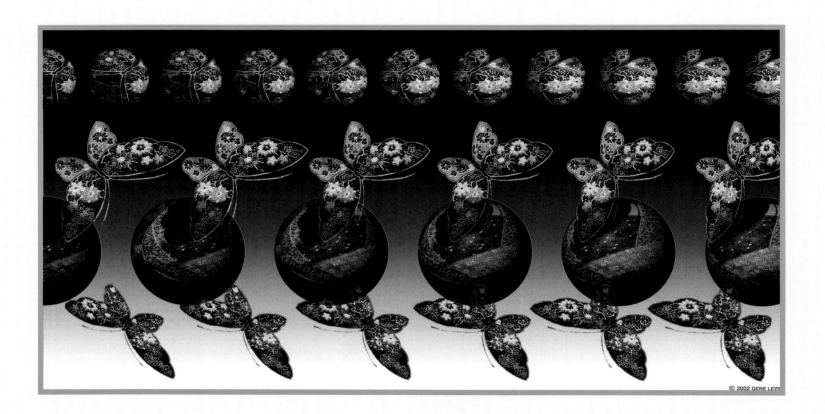

© 2002 GENE LEVI

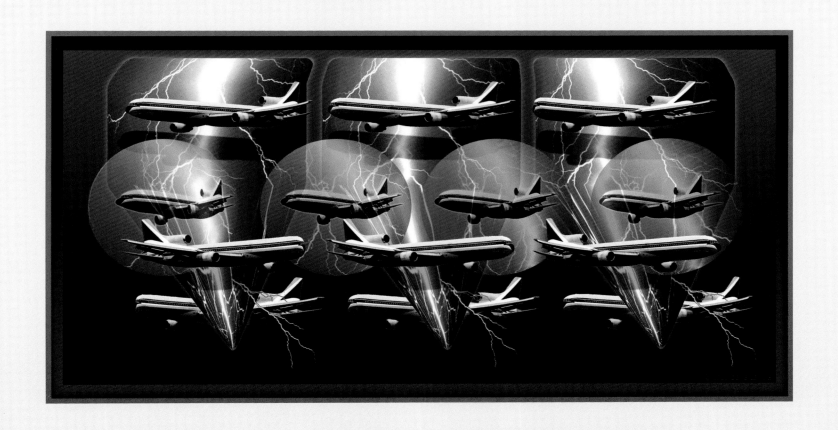

Pyramid Valley

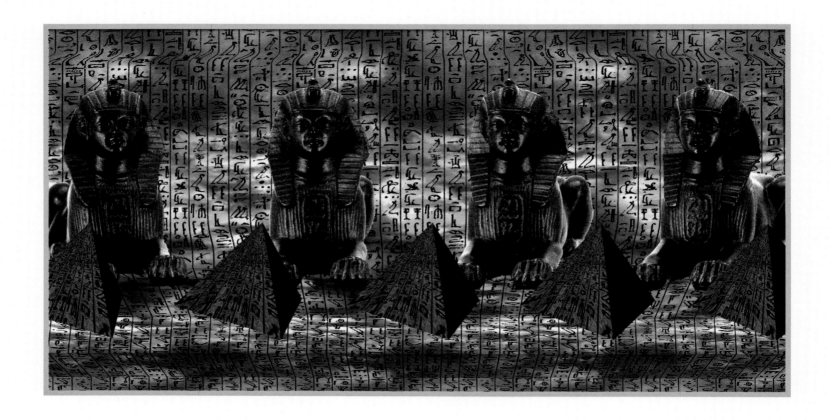

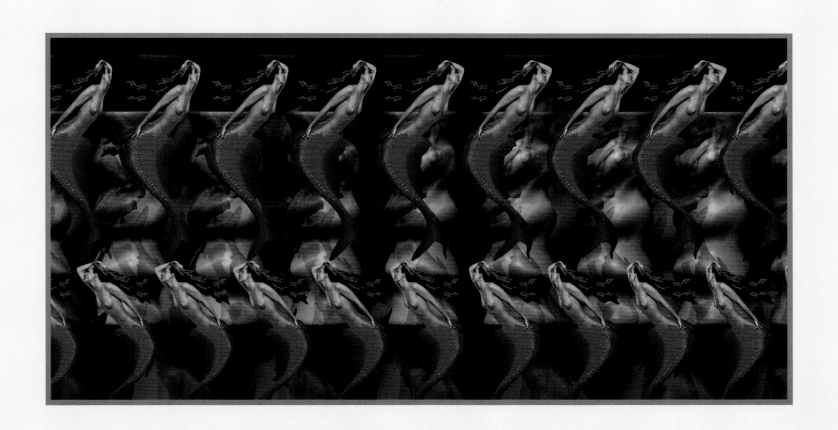

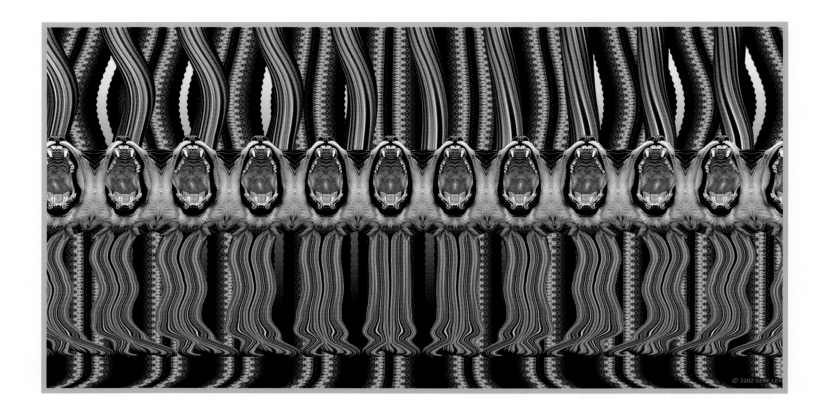

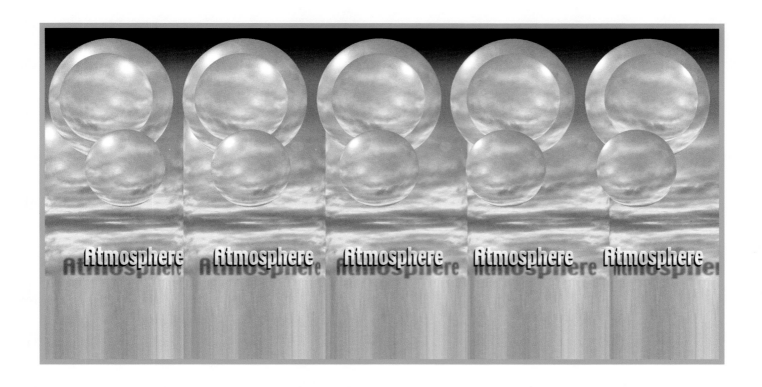

© 2001 GENE LEVINE

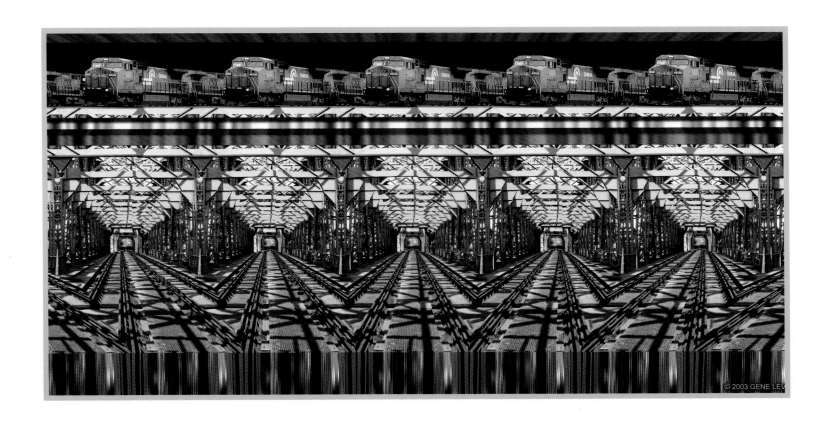

© 2003 GENE LEV

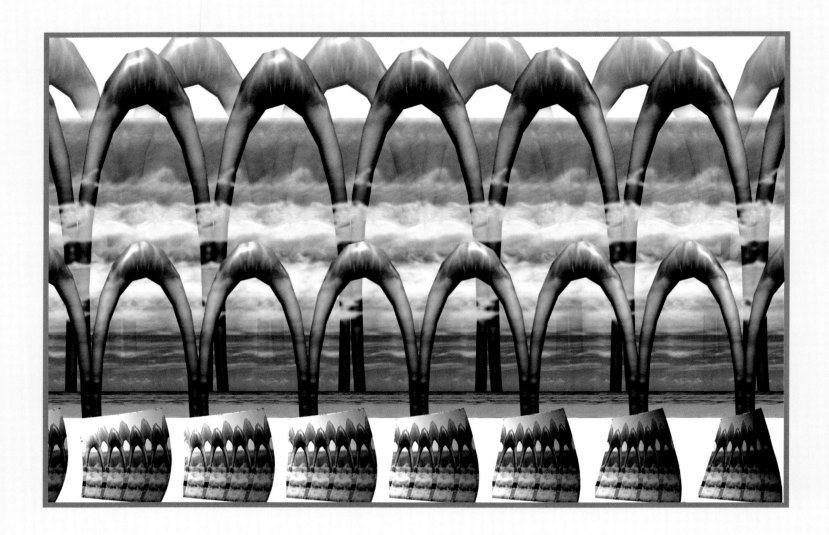

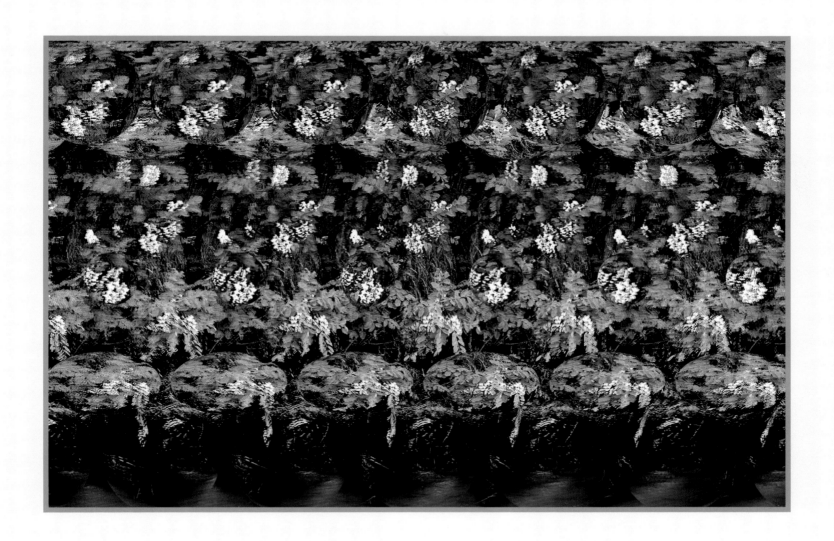

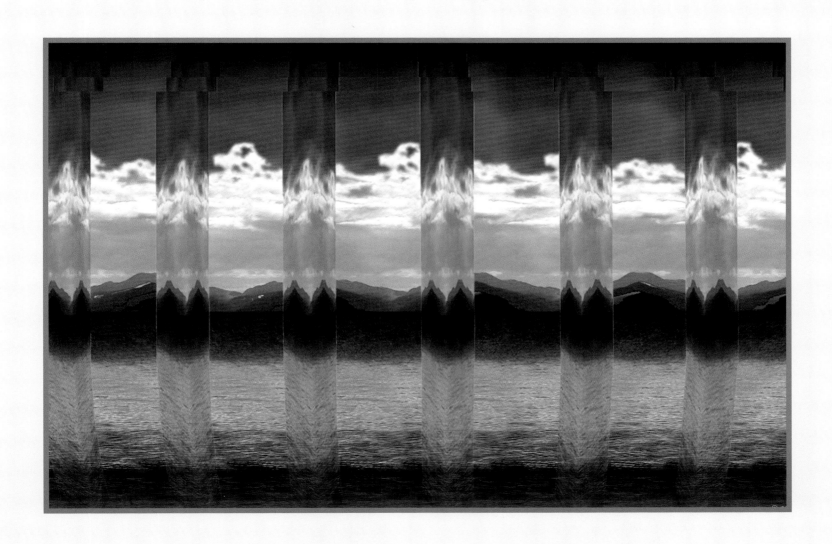

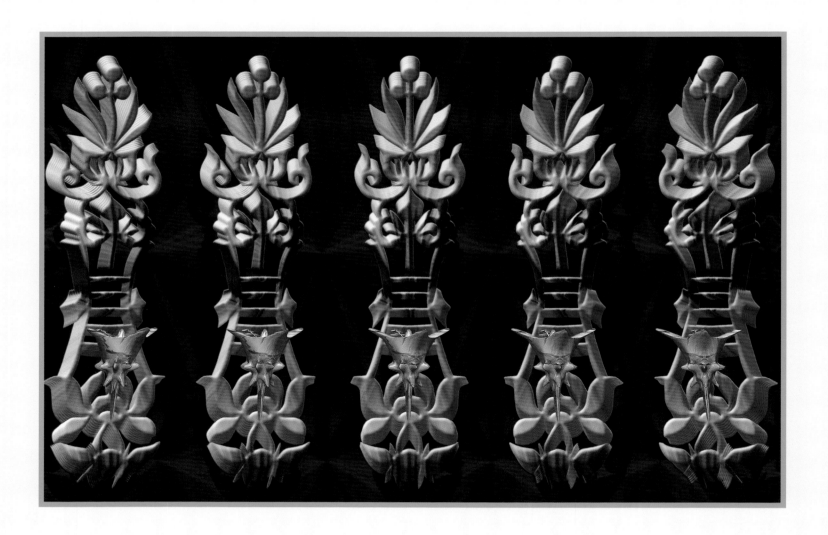

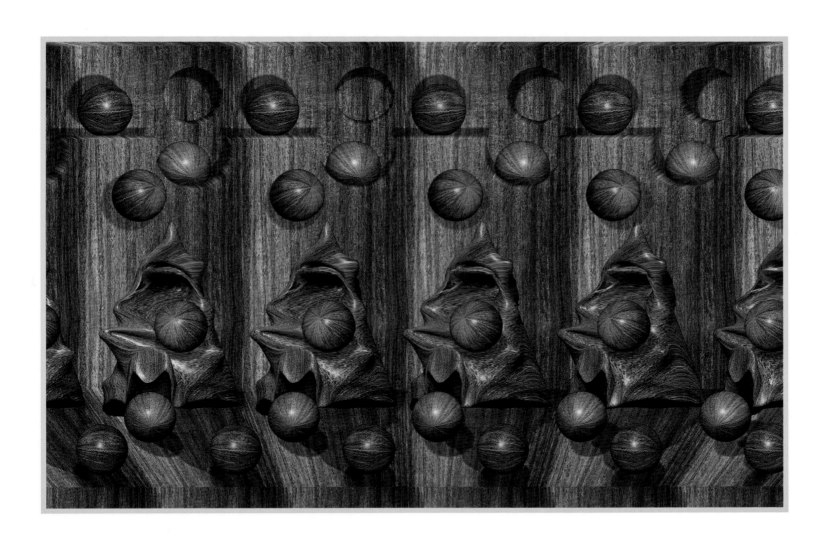

Sunflower

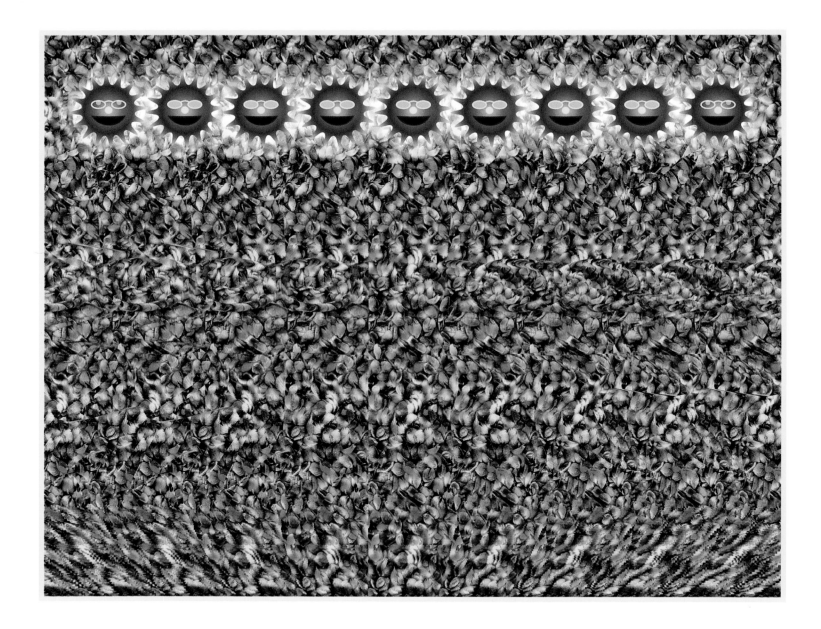

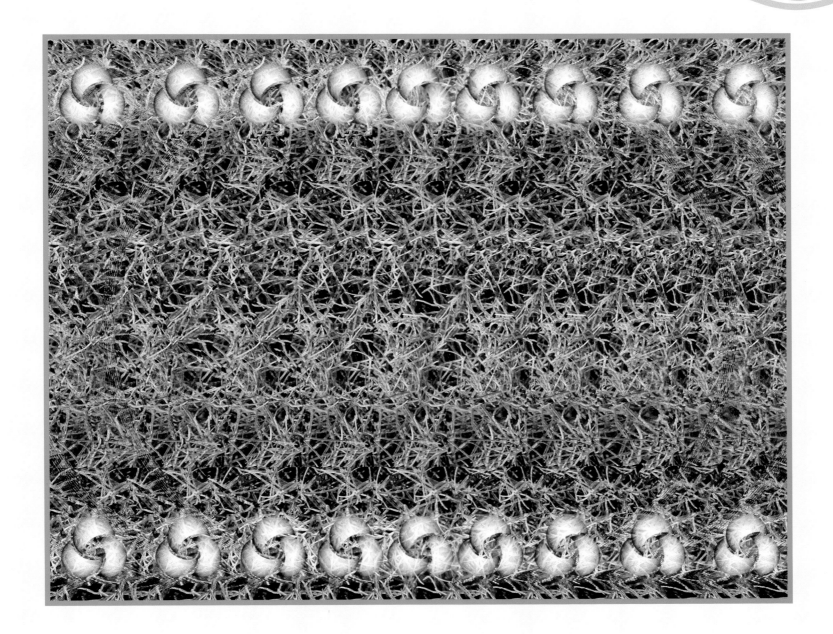

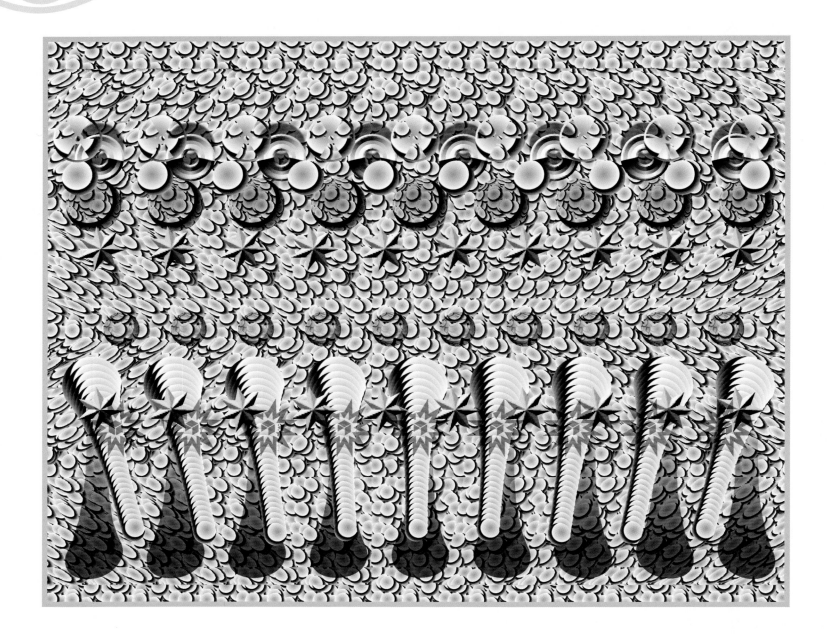

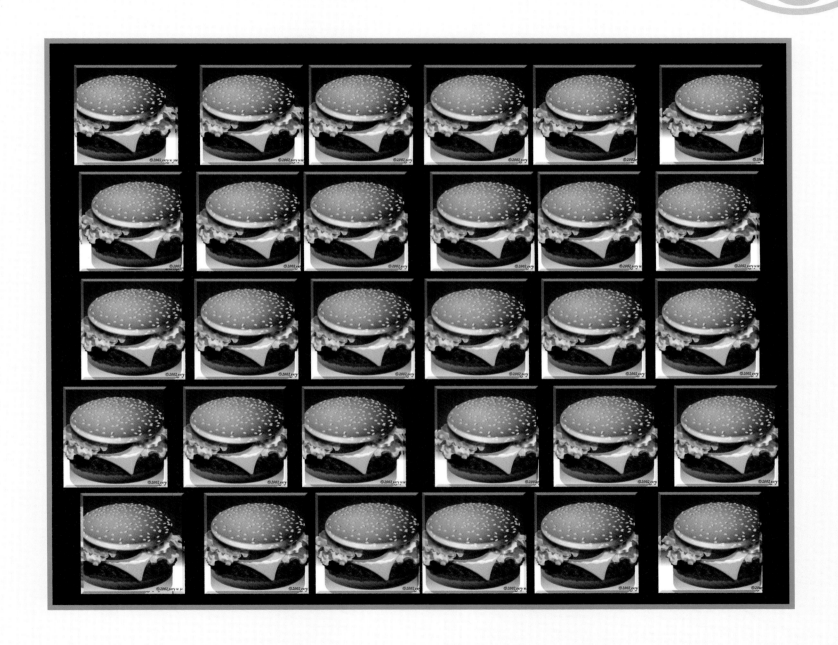

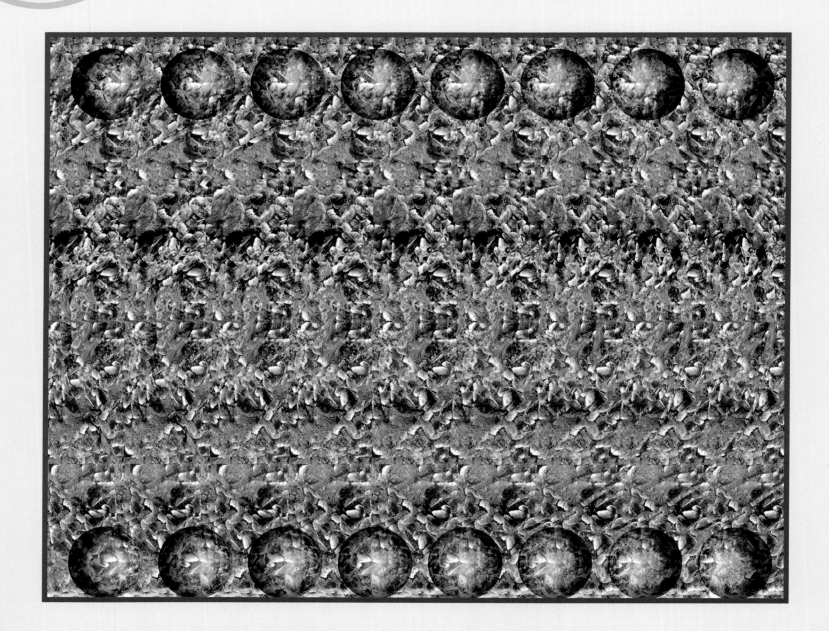

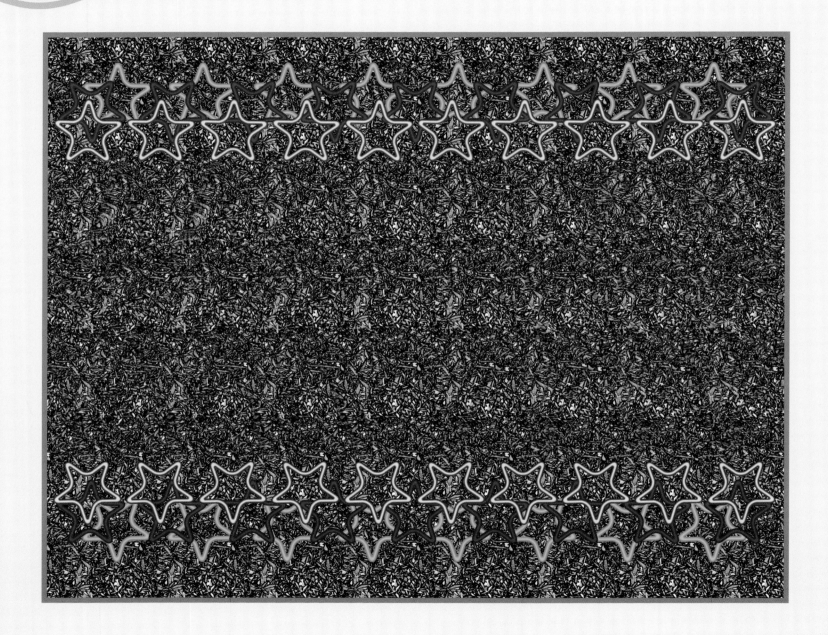

Pluses

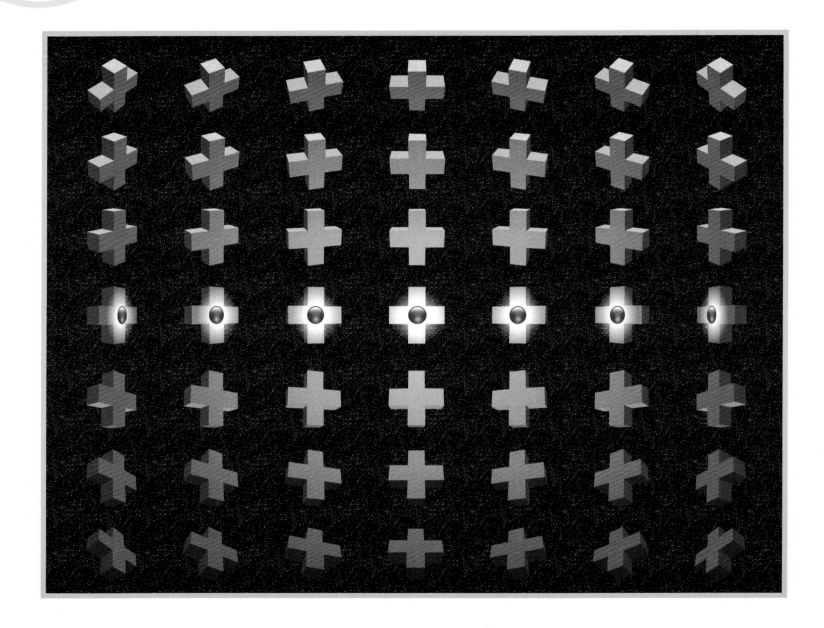

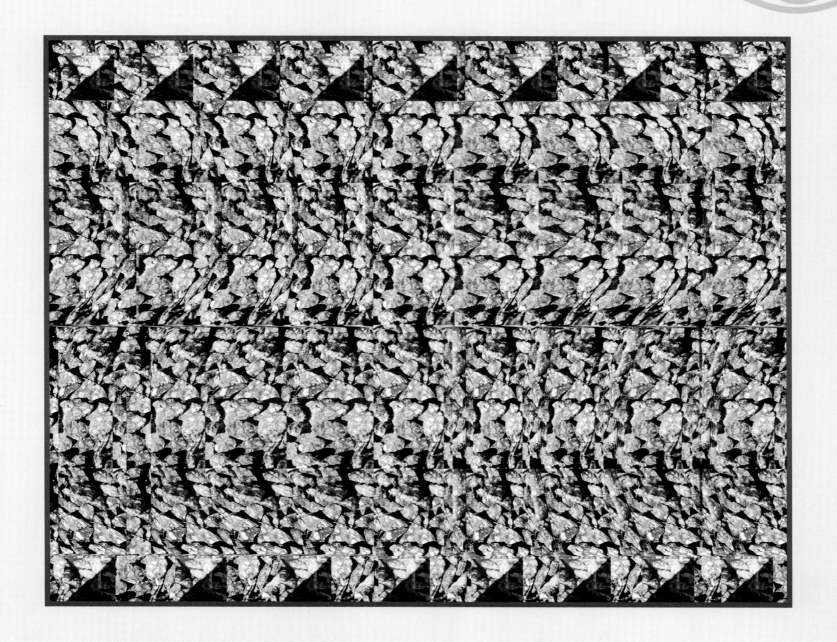

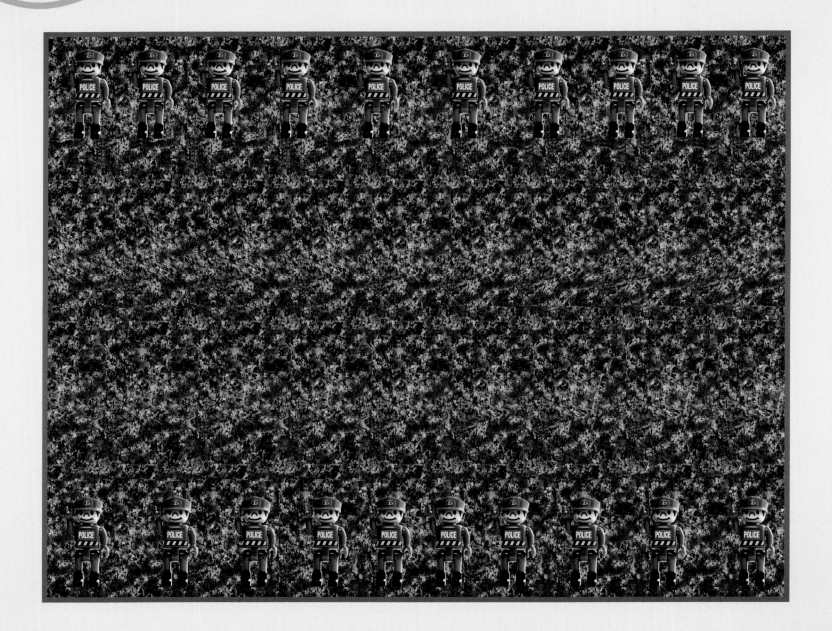

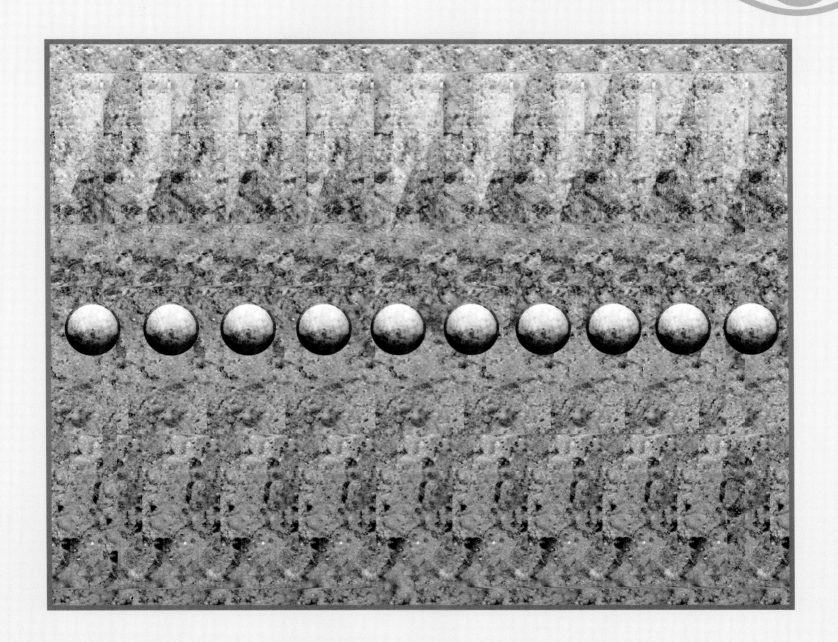

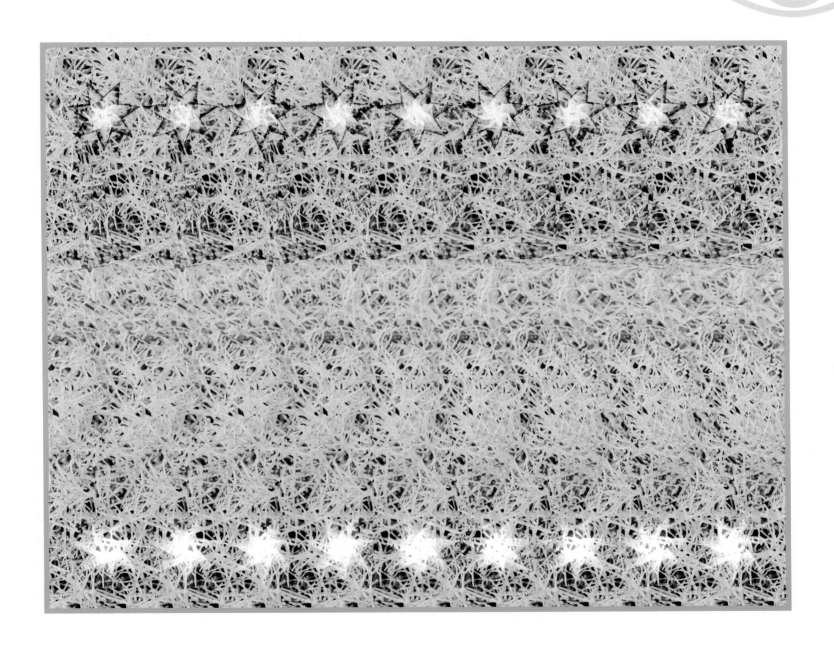

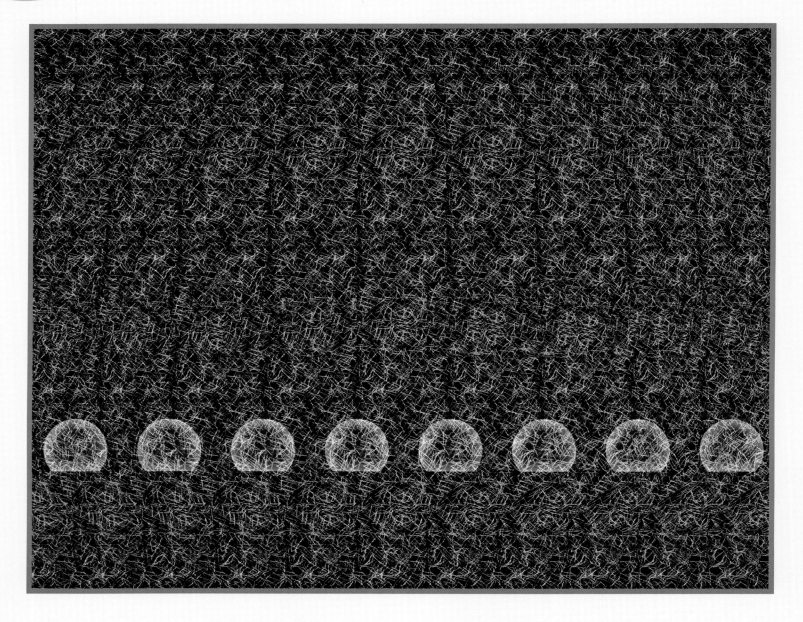

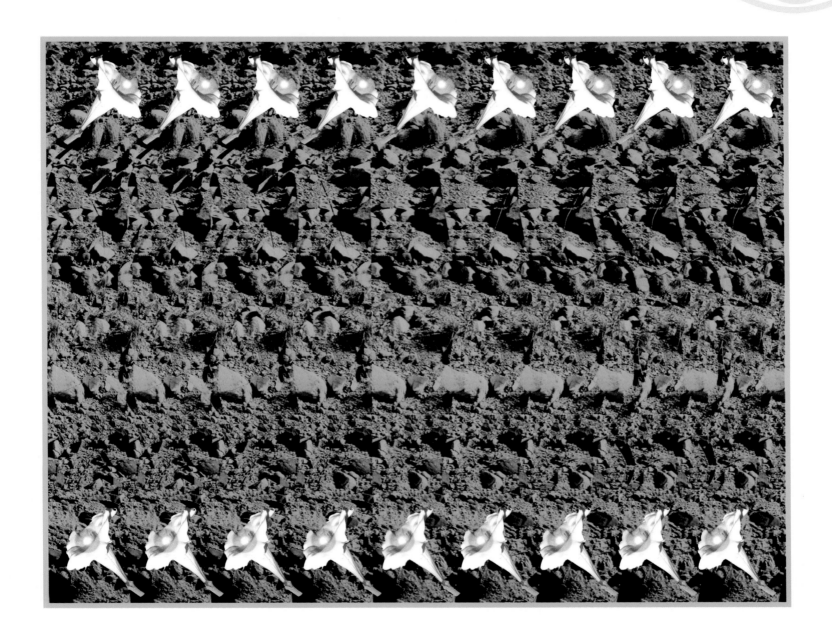

Cube & Hoop

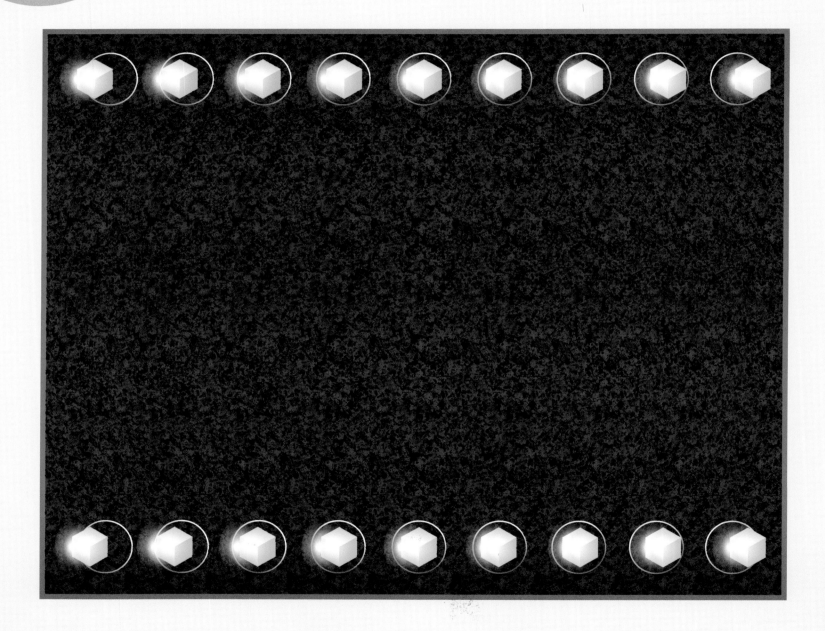

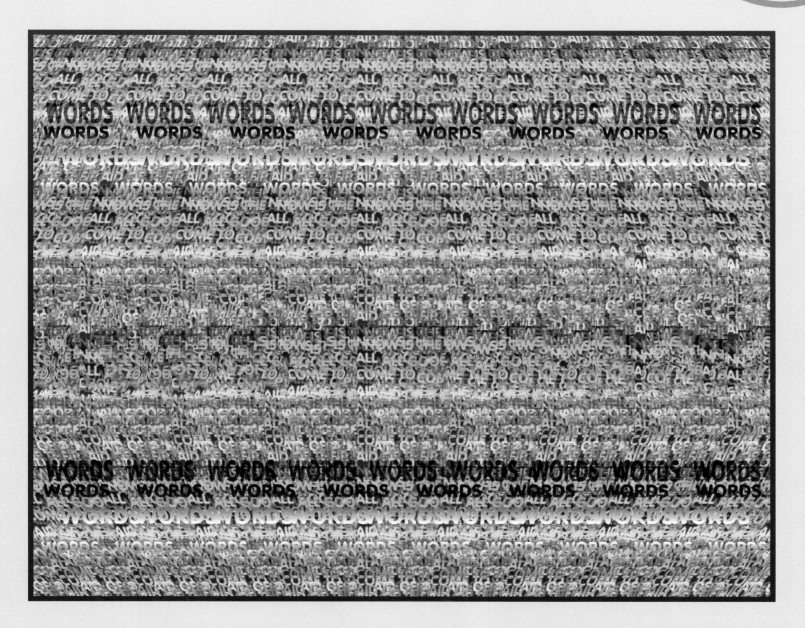

© 2004 GENE LEVINE

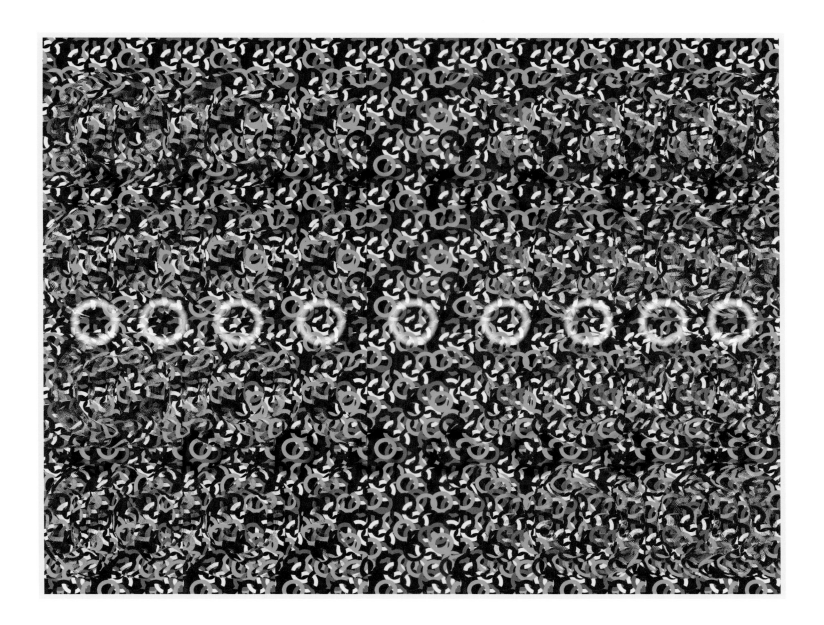

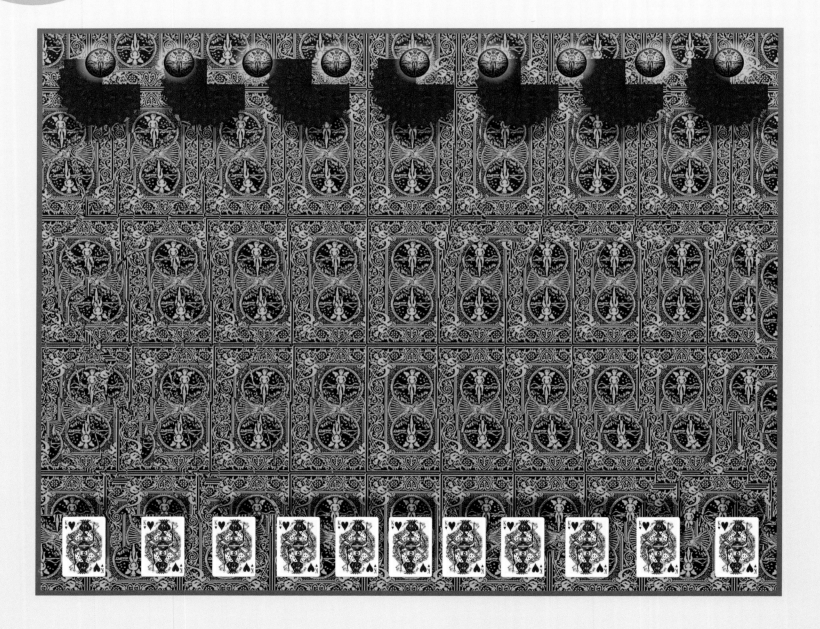

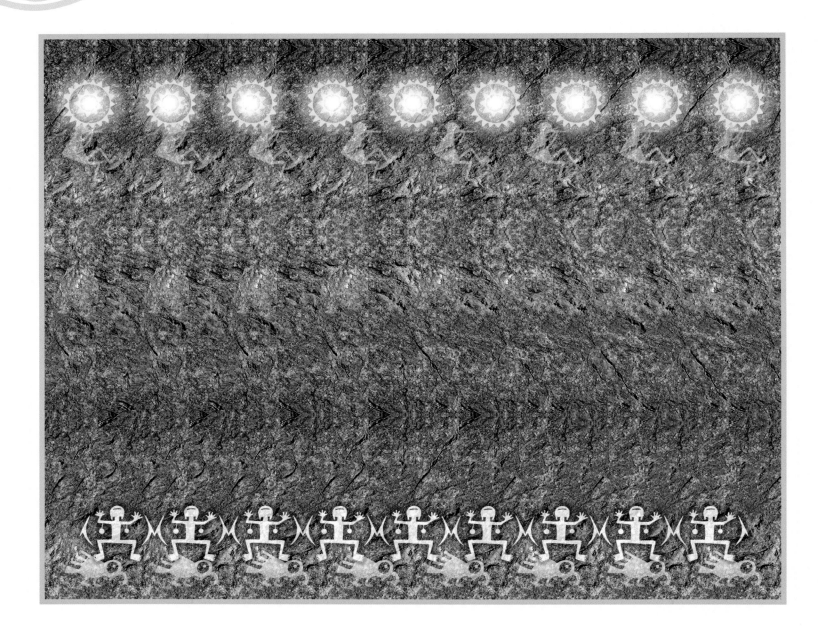

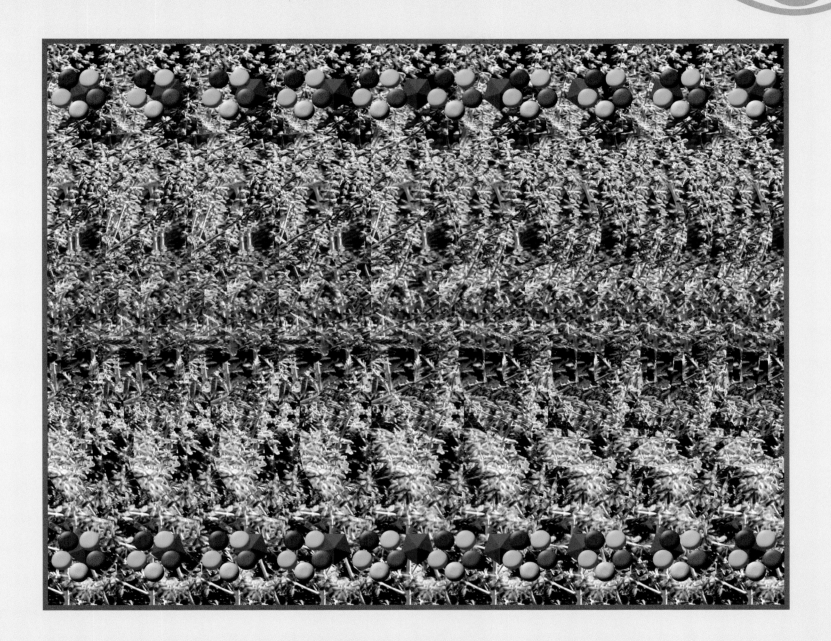

Organic Vacuum

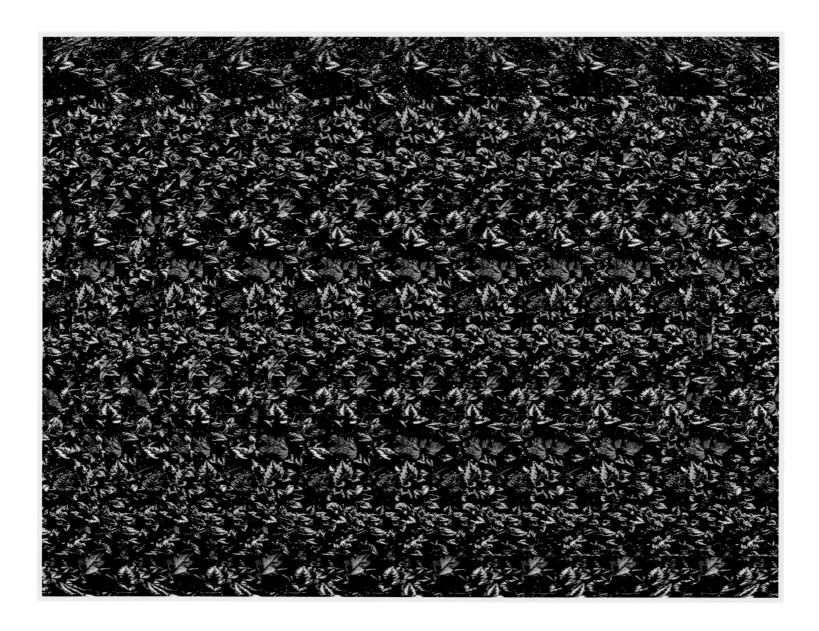

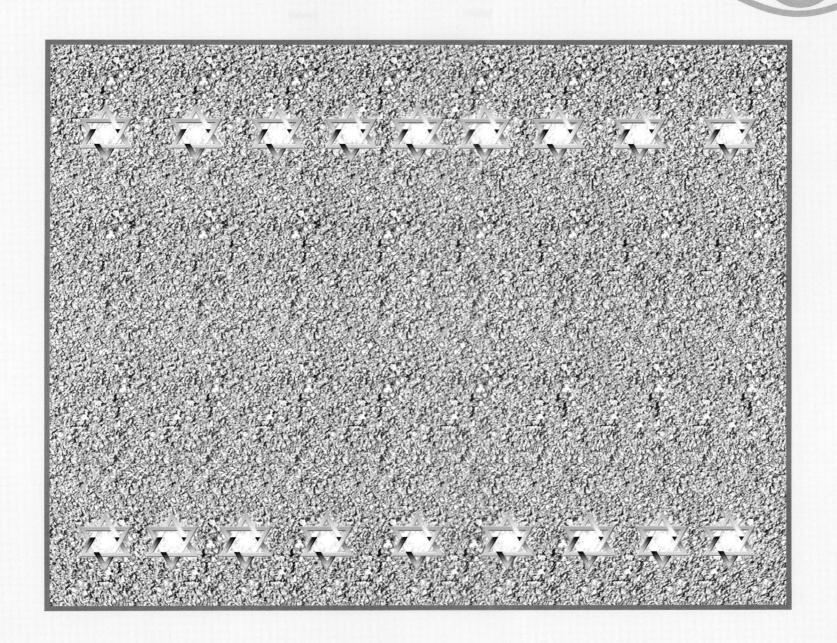

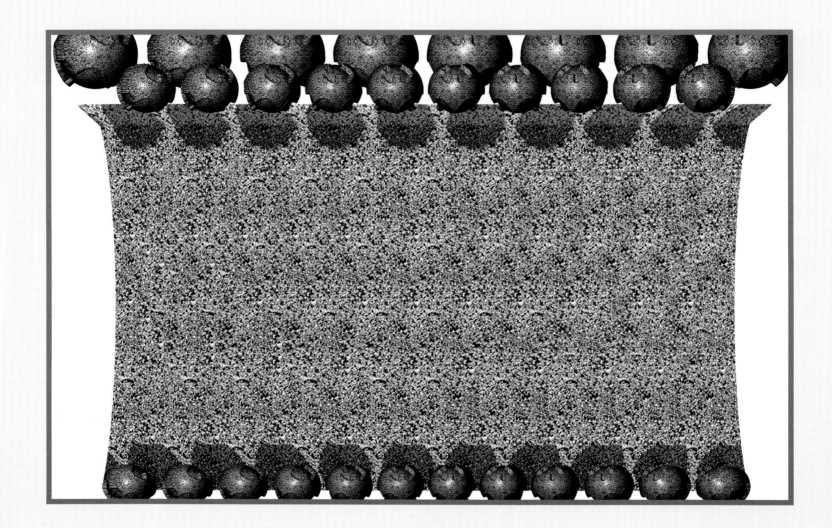

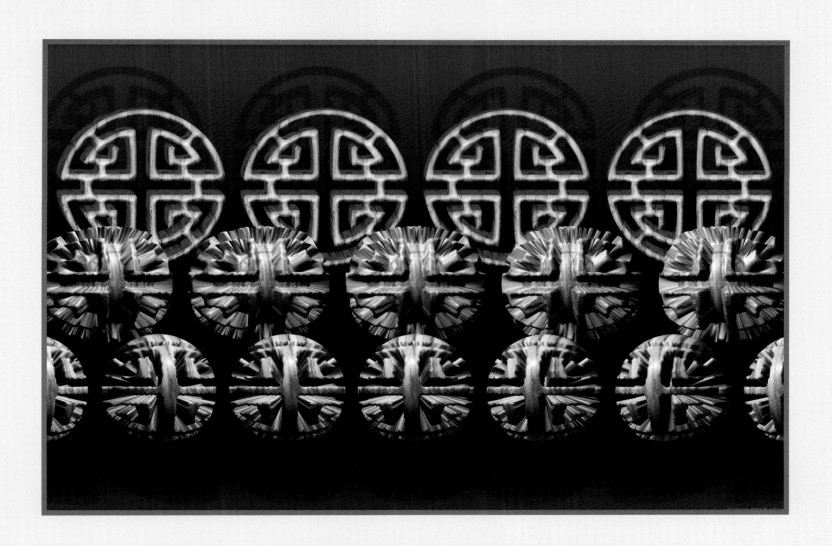

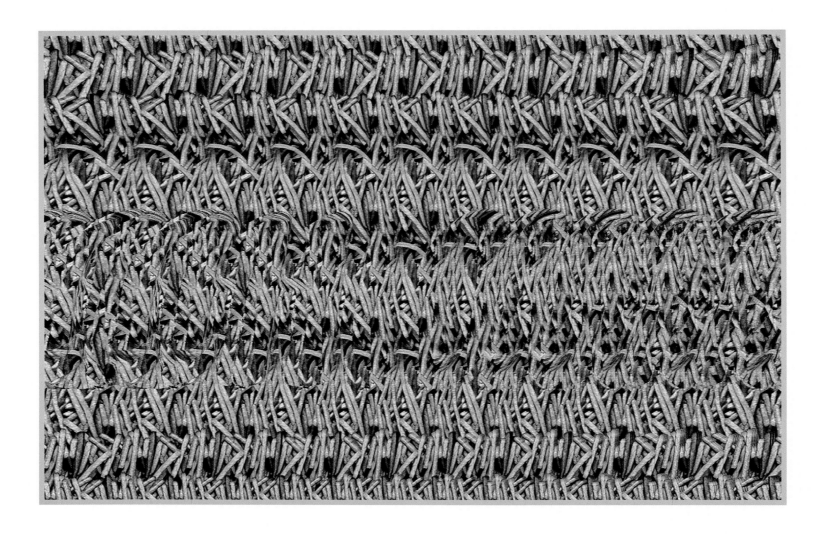

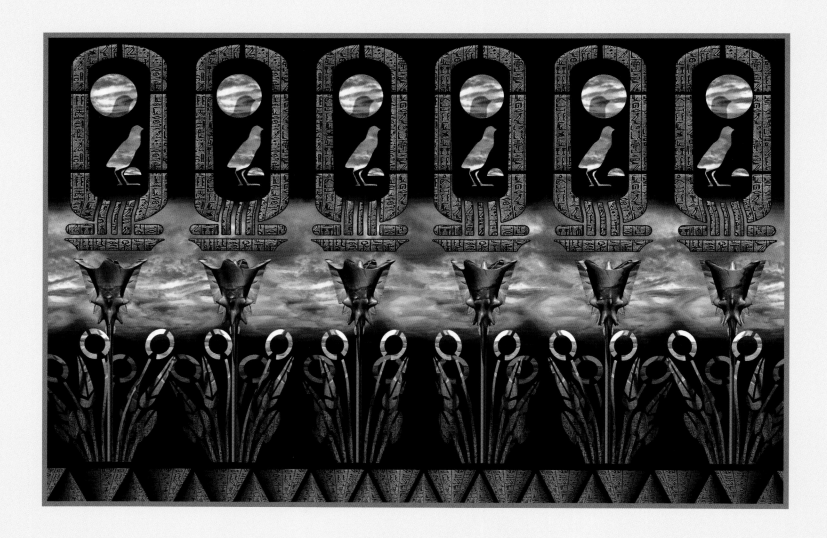

© 2004 GENE

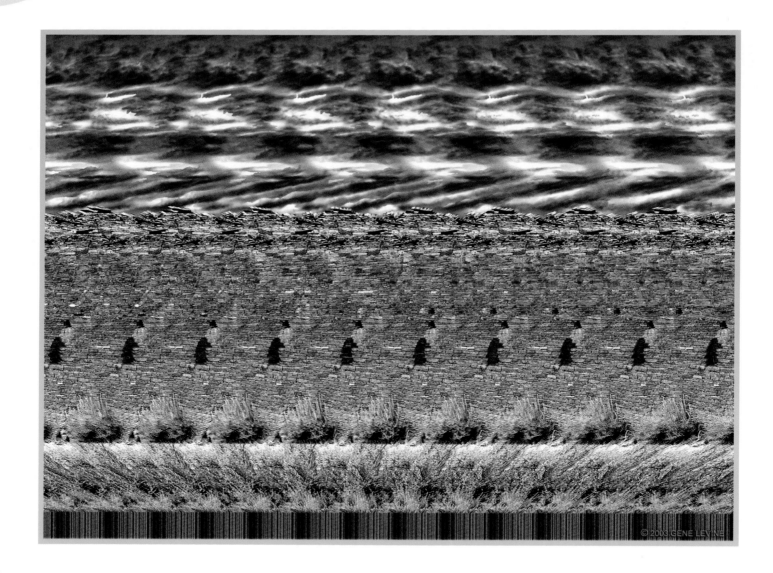

© 2003 GENE LEVINE

© 2003 GENE LEVINE

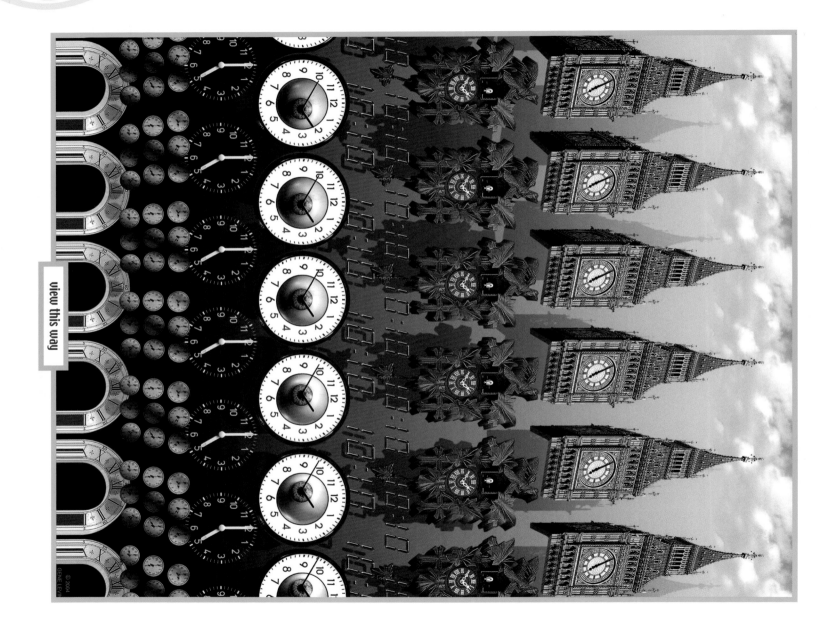

view this way

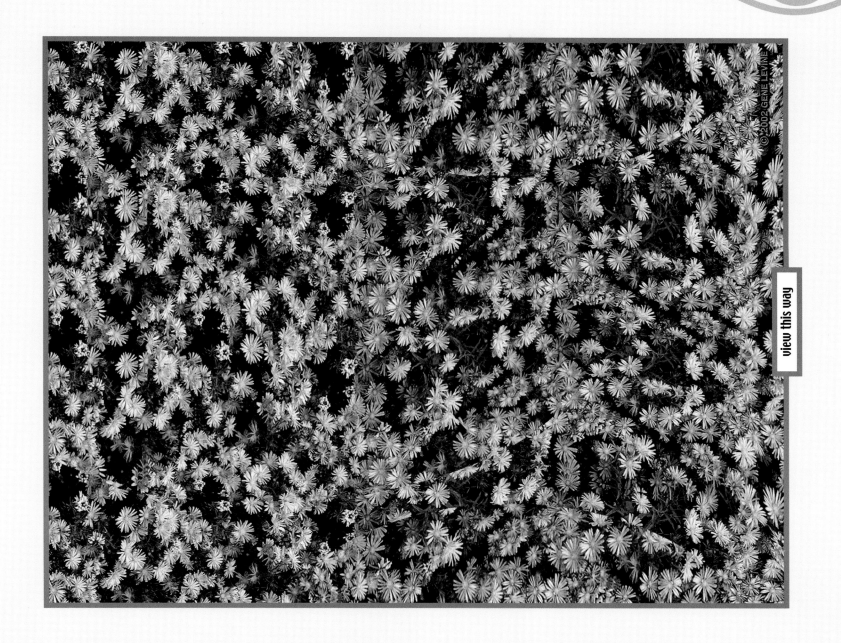

© 2002 GENE LEVINE

view this way

view this way

© 2004 GENE L

view this way

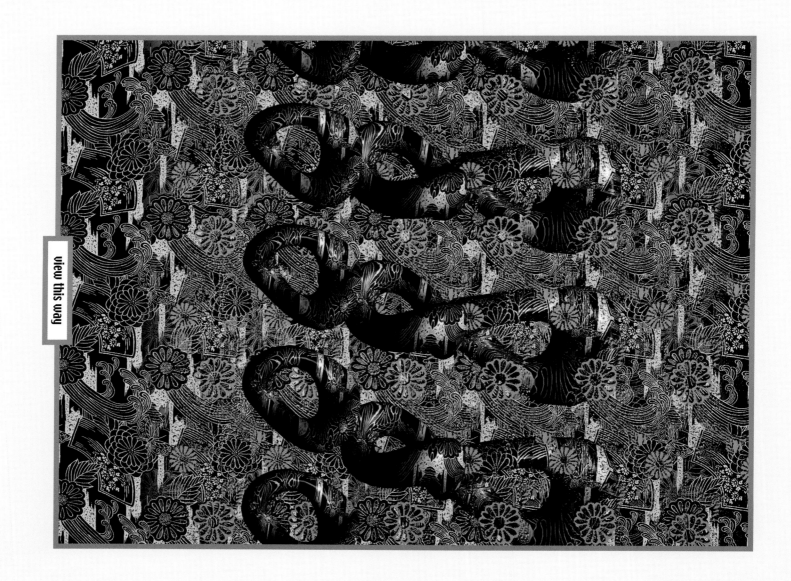

view this way

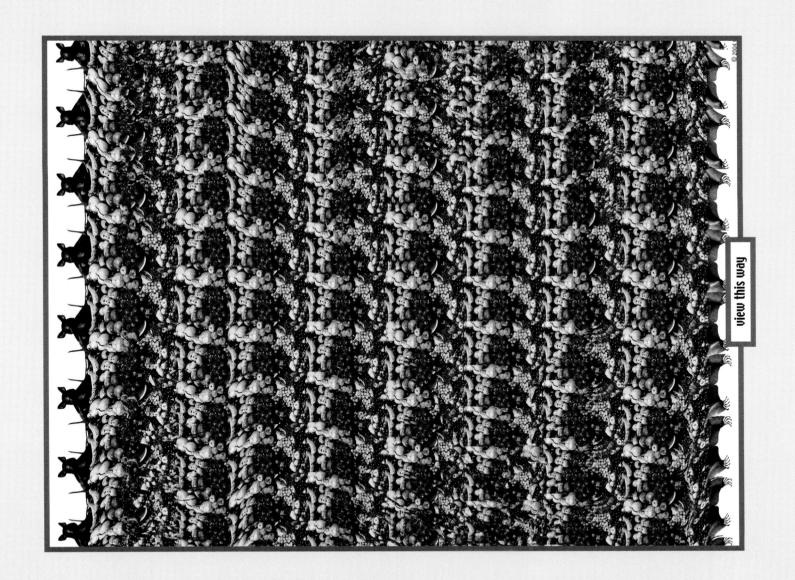

view this way

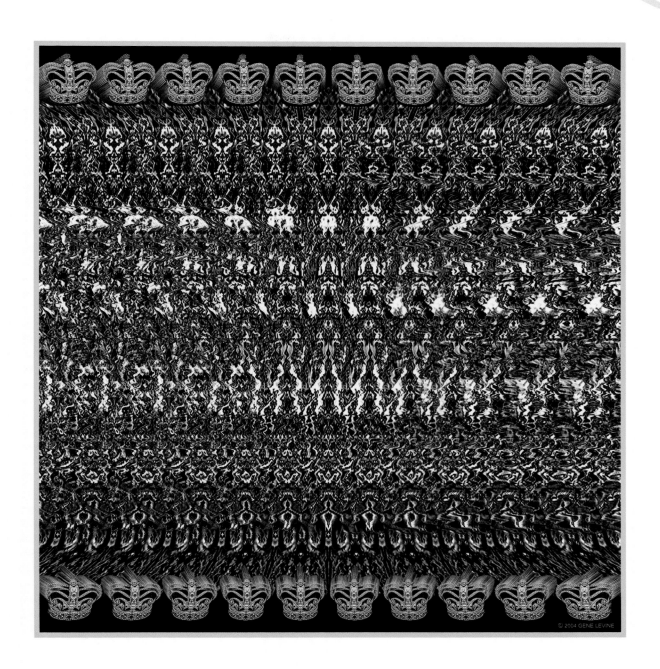

© 2004 GENE LEVINE

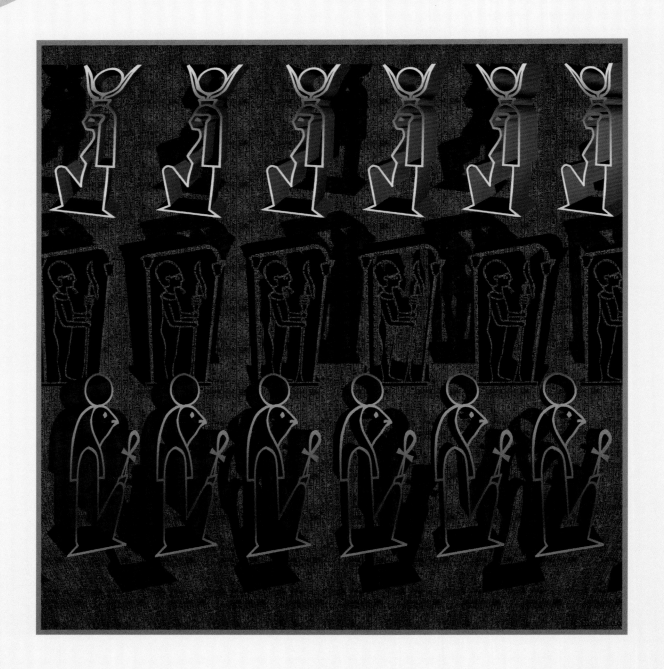

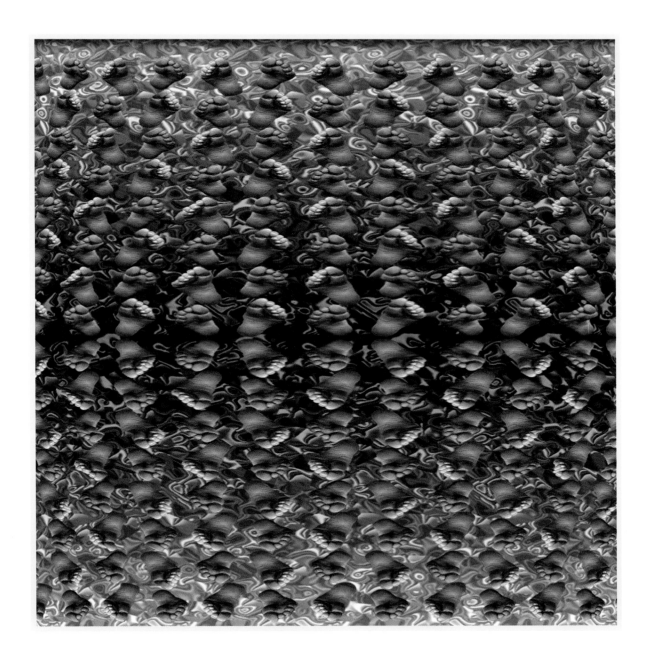

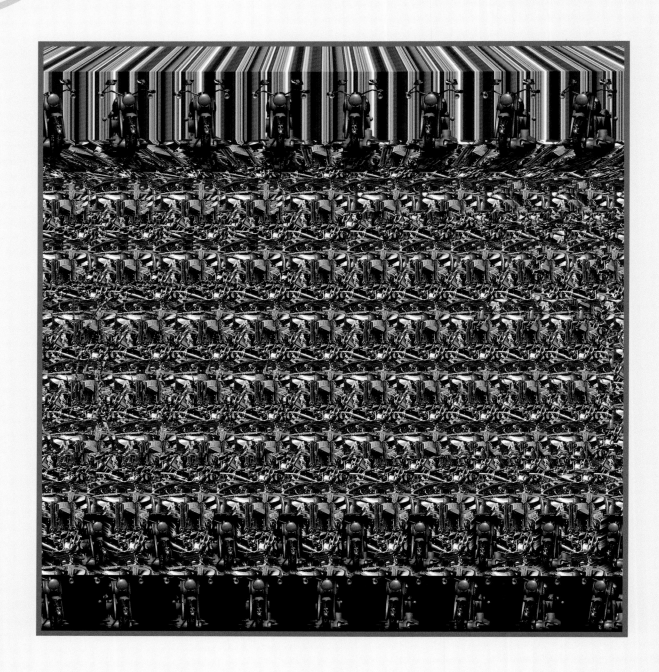

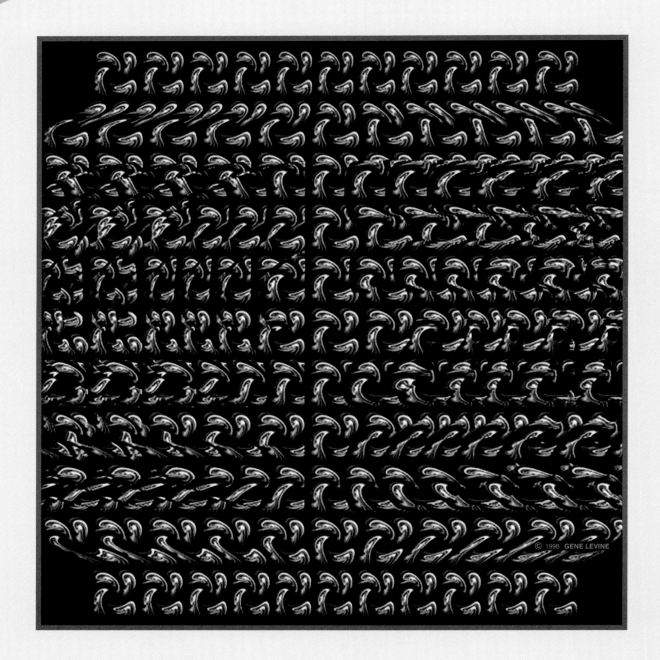

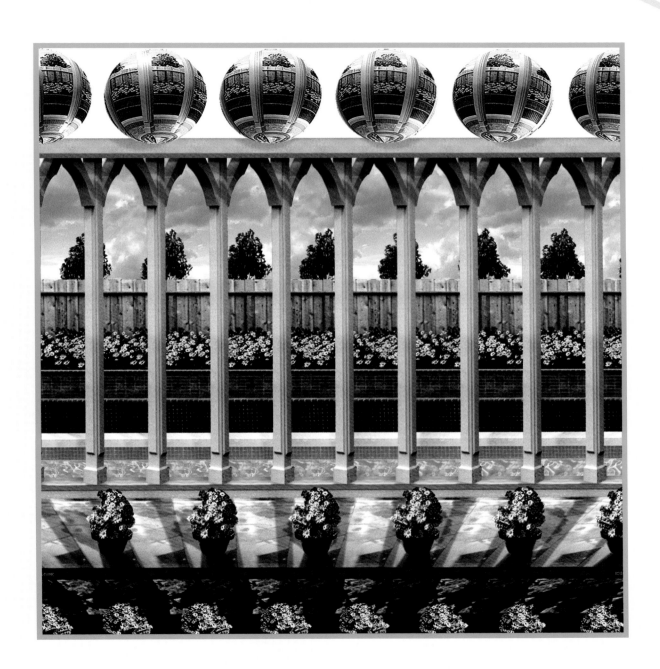

© 2001 GENE LEVINE

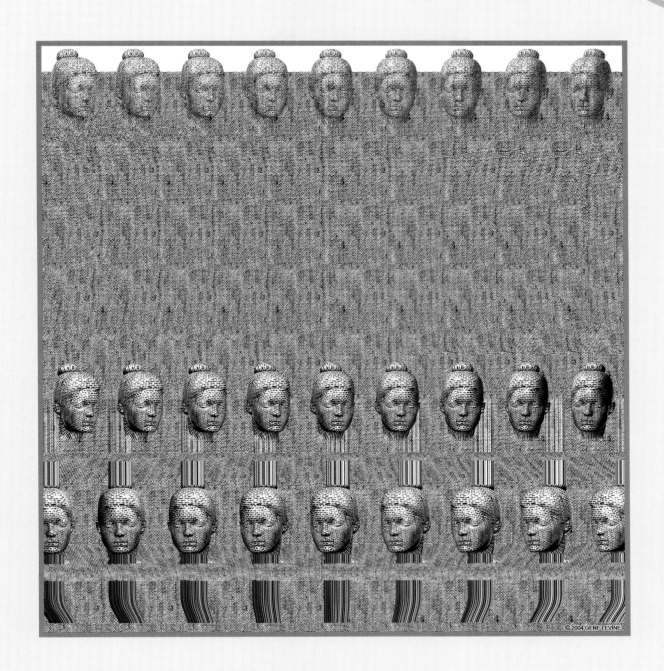

© 2004 GENE LEVINE

Revelations

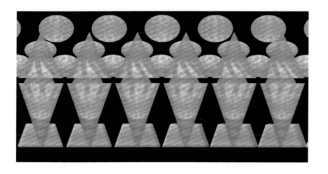

page 8   Byzantine Crystal

page 9   Edge of the Woods

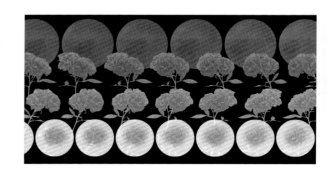

page 10   Rose Rows

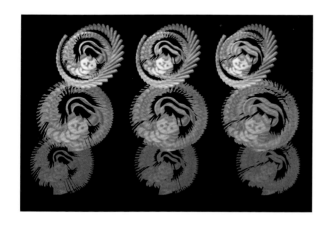

page 11   Scorpions

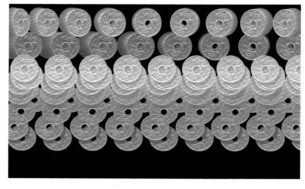

page 12   Four Hundred 50 Yen

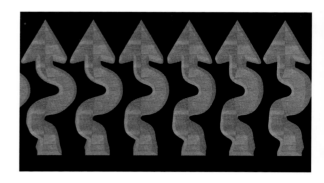

page 13   Straight as an Arrow

138

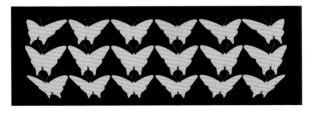

page 14   Blue Butterfly

page 15   Butterfly Lines

page 16   Diamonds in the Rough

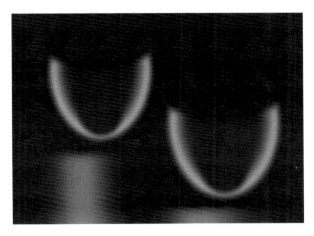

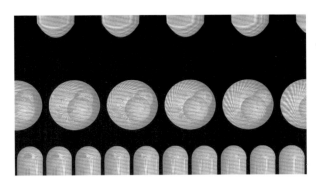

page 17   Dragonfly Sparks

page 18   Johnny's Garden

page 19   Frax Bubbles

Revelations

page 20   Butterfly Pillows

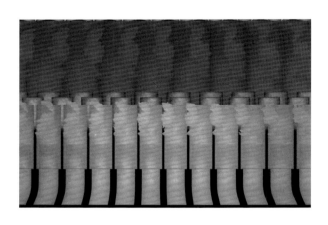

page 21   Cloud Funnels

page 22   Colour Sieve

page 23   Dragon Light

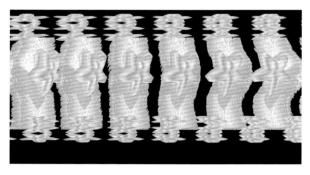

page 24   Molten Water

page 25   Mixed Vegetables

page 26   Star Screen

page 27   Star Family

page 28   Man & Woman

page 29   Making Honey

page 30   Hidden Image

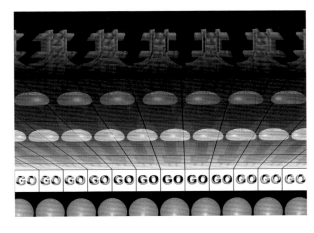

page 31   GO

Revelations

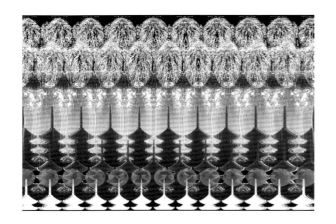

page 32   Fireworks

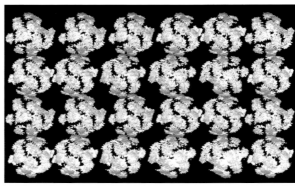

page 33   Floral Twists

page 34   Footprints

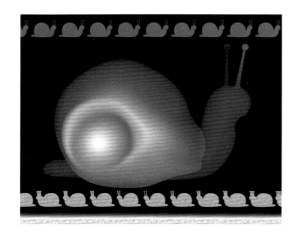

page 35   Escargot

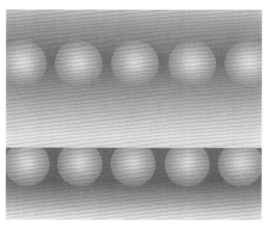

page 36   Gold Eye Sky

page 37   Goldfish

Revelations

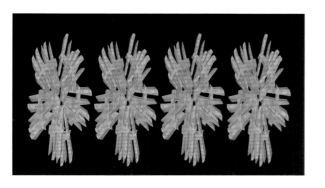

page 38   Stone Burst

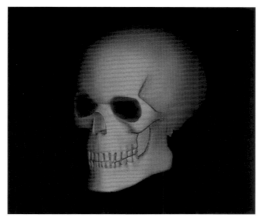

page 39   The Phrenologist

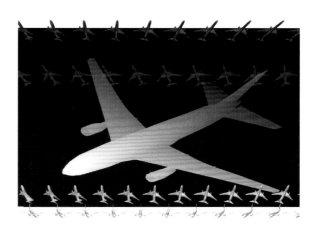

page 40   Takeoff & Landing

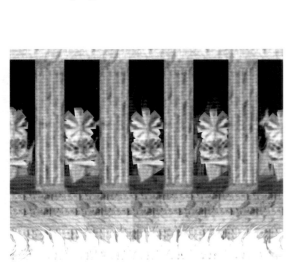

page 41   Temple Albathor

page 42   Heart in Heart

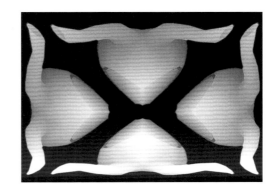

page 43   Heart-throb

Revelations

page 44   Terraced

page 45   The Guardian

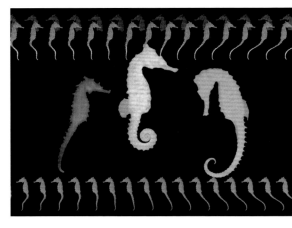

page 46   Seahorse Herd

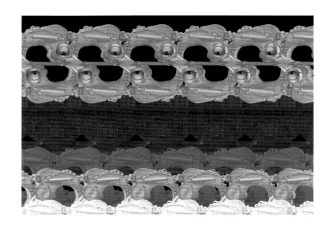

page 47   The Stereogram Machine

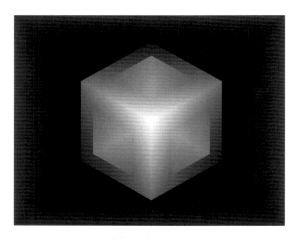

page 48   Box in a Box

page 49   Butterfly

Revelations

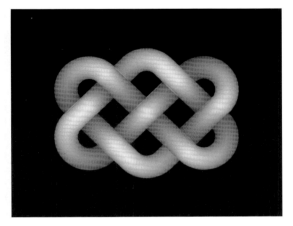

page 50   Celtic Knot

page 51   Comedy

page 52   Dice

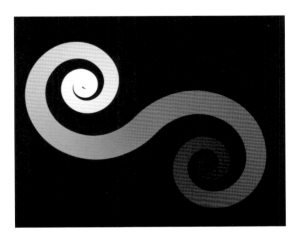

page 53   Double Spiral

page 54   Dos Espirales

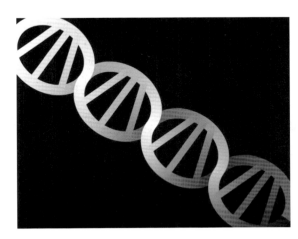

page 55   DNA

Revelations

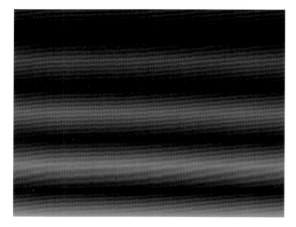

page 56   Fantasy Nouveau

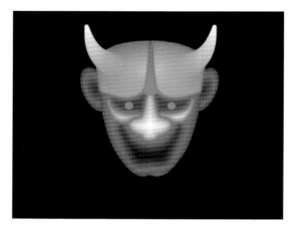

page 57   Han-nya

page 58   Hello

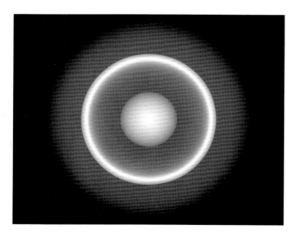

page 59   Inverted Spheres

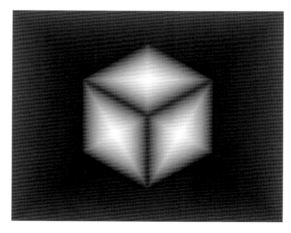

page 60   Indented Cubes

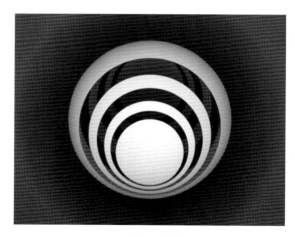

page 61   Rings

page 62   Lock & Key

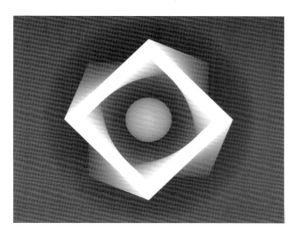

page 63   Mystic Shapes

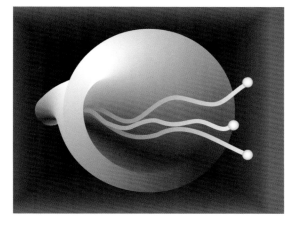

page 64   An Interesting Shape

page 65   Hot-Air Balloon

page 66   Entanglements

page 67   Shamrock

Revelations

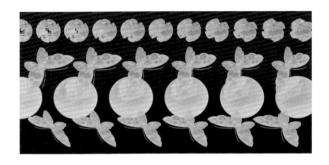

page 68   Butterfly Scarf

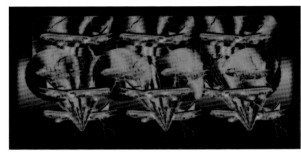

page 69   Holding Pattern

page 70   Pyramid Valley

page 71   Yang Yin

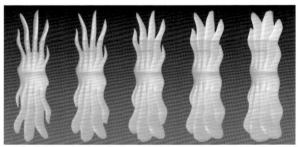

page 72   Swimming Ocean

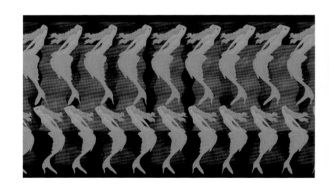

page 73   Mermaid

Revelations

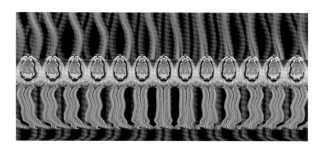

page 74   Uproar

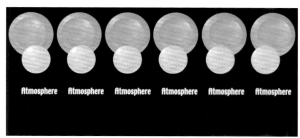

page 75   Atmosphere

page 76   Sunset

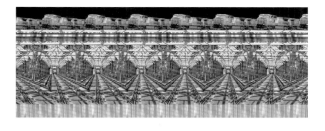

page 77   End of the Line

page 78   Sea Palace

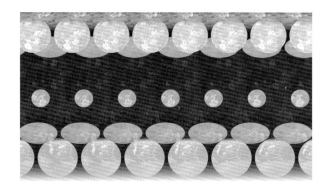

page 79   River Canopy

Revelations

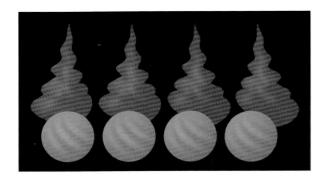

page 80   Inspiration

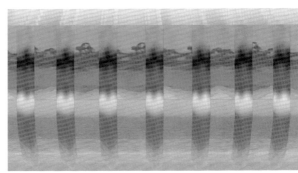

page 81   Palais du Lac

page 82   Lotus Garden

page 83   Koa Construction

page 84   Sunflower

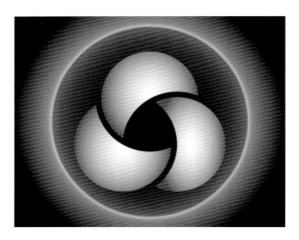

page 85   Trilogy 1

Revelations

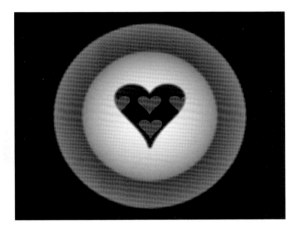

page 86   Hole in My Heart

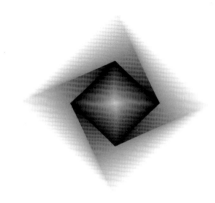

page 87   Hole in the Desert

page 88   Golden Medley

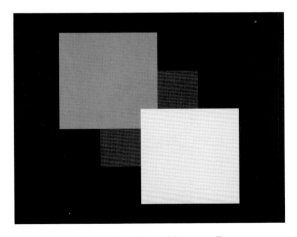

page 89   Floating Cheese Burgers

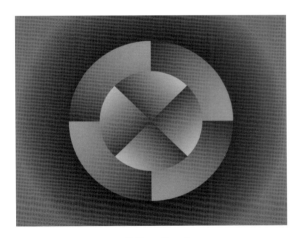

page 90   Equinox

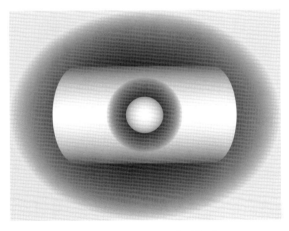

page 91   Grass Cylinder

Revelations

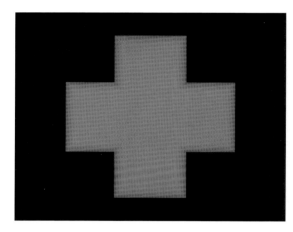

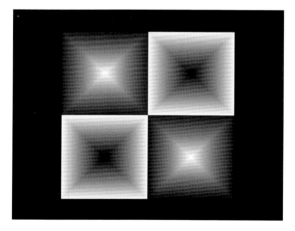

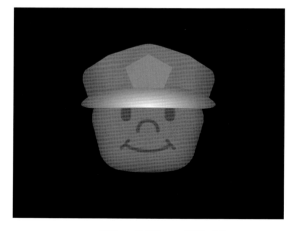

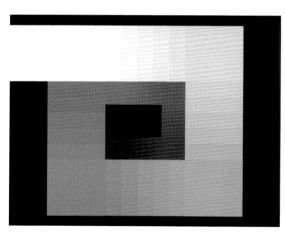

Revelations

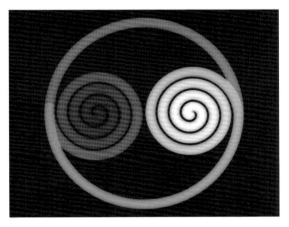

page 98   Spirals – In & Out

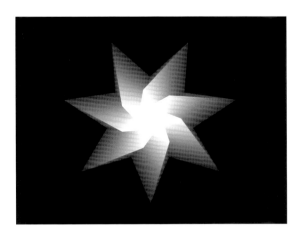

page 99   Twisting Star

page 100   Window

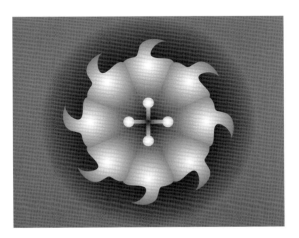

page 101   Desert Flower

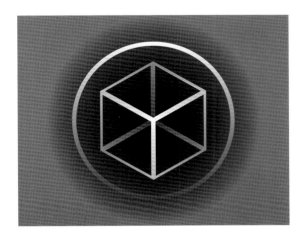

page 102   Cube & Hoop

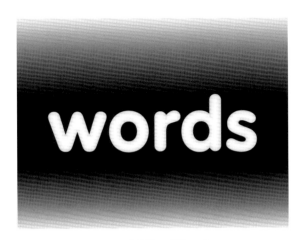

page 103   Words

Revelations

page 104   Winter Trees

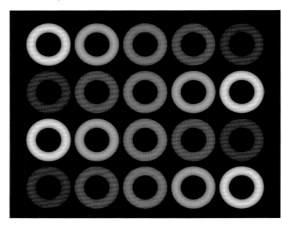

page 105   Circles

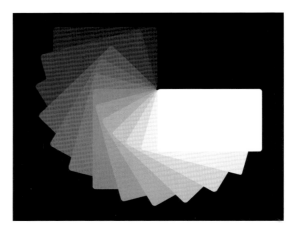

page 106   Cards

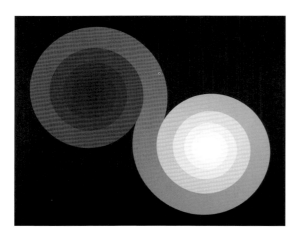

page 107   Artemisia Spirals

page 108   Anasazi Petroglyphs

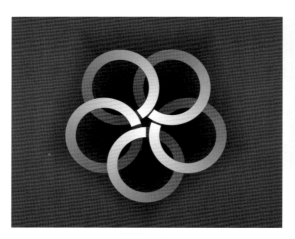

page 109   5 Rings

page 110   Organic Vacuum

page 111   Star of David

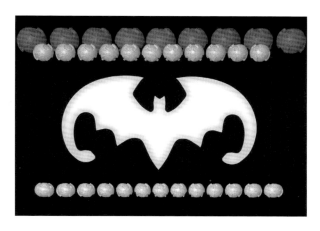

page 112   Granite Fu

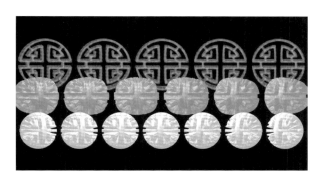

page 113   Jade Riches

page 114   French Chow

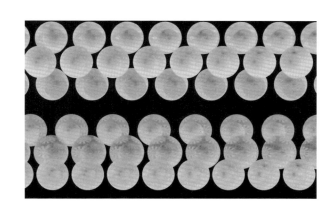

page 115   Enbubbled

Revelations

page 116   Sunset on the Nile

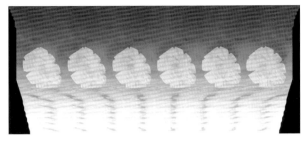

page 117   Rising Sun

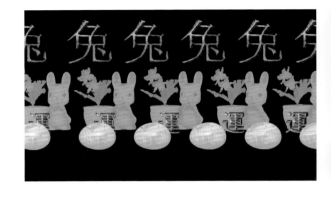

page 118   Lucky Rabbit

page 119   Mesa Verde

page 120   New Mexico

page 121   Open the Door

Revelations

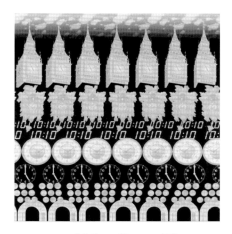

page 122   Stereo Time

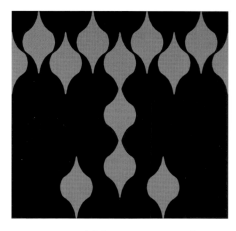

page 123   Aster Turf

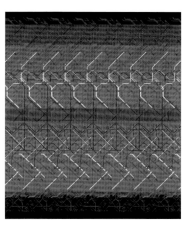

page 124   London Disconnect

page 125   Shamrocks

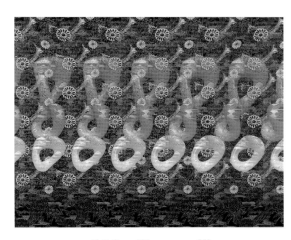

page 126   Blossom Waves

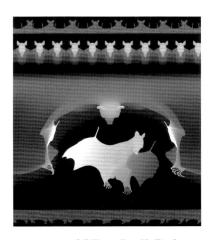

page 127   Fruit Bat

Revelations

page 128   Cherry Blossom

page 129   Crown Thee

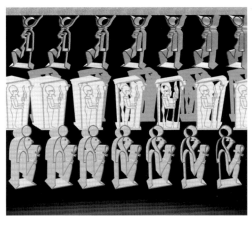

page 130   Egyptian Shadows

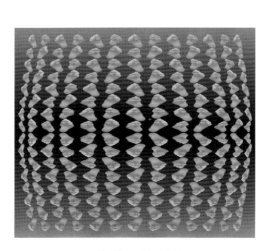

page 131   Footsteps

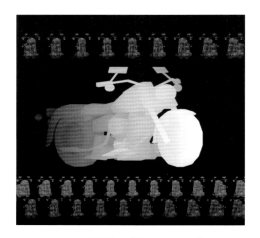

page 132   Stereocycle

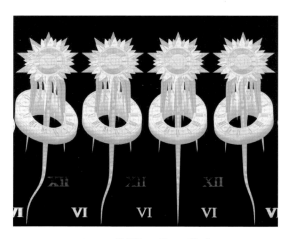

page 133   Sundial

Revelations

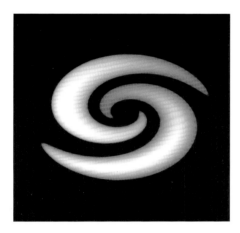

page 134   Wing Wang

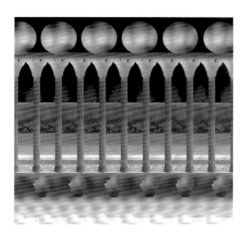

page 135   The Yard

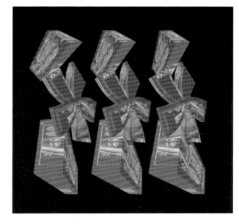

page 136   King & Queen

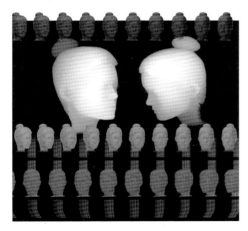

page 137   Head Bands